**calorie** and **fat** unit counter

Rebecca Rose

## What are Slim•Fast meal replacements?

Each Slim•Fast meal replacement has been developed by nutritionists to provide a balanced, nutritious meal of 200–250 calories. They meet the recommended standards for protein and micronutrients, with 23 vitamins and minerals and essential fatty acids. It would be virtually impossible to prepare a conventional meal with the same nutrition in so few calories!

So, with Slim•Fast meal replacements you can follow a calorie-reduced diet without the hassle of weighing and measuring every meal, because most of it's done for you, and you're taking in the recommended level of essential micronutrients, as well as protein and fibre.

And they're so convenient – the perfect solution for a healthy meal on the run. The ready to drink shakes and meal replacement bars are great for a day out, and the soups and pasta require nothing more than a kettle and a bowl.

## Calories – the bit about arithmetic

To lose weight, you need to take in fewer calories than you use up.

It's simple arithmetic: 1lb (0.5kg) of body fat equals around 3,500 calories. So you need to create a deficit of 500 calories a day to lose 1lb (0.5kg) in a week – or 1000 calories a day to lose 2lbs (1kg) a week. A 1–2lb (0.5–1kg) weight loss per week is a good goal. More than this requires a drastic change in eating patterns, which is difficult to keep up and can present health risks.

The Slim•Fast Plan is designed to cut your calorie intake to between 1200–1400 a day, without lots of fiddly calorie counting, so you should be able to lose weight steadily.

# CONTENTS

|  | Calories | Fat (g) |
|---|---|---|

## SNACKS

### Sweet

| | Calories | Fat (g) |
|---|---|---|
| *1 Small banana sliced with Butterscotch Sauce (5g)* | 105 | 2 |
| *1 Sliced apple sprinkled with 1 tsp cinnamon* | 77 | 0 |
| *Fruit Salad – satsuma, grapes (40g portion),* | | |
| *1/2 kiwi fruit, 1 passion fruit* | 104 | 0 |
| *Cherries (200g portion)* | 106 | 0 |
| *1/2 grapefruit with 1 tsp sugar* | 94 | 0 |
| *Watermelon (300g slice)* | 96 | 0 |
| *One box of raisins (40g)* | 109 | 0 |
| *3 whole dried apricots* | 94 | 0 |
| *4 dried prunes and 4 dried figs* | 88 | 1 |
| *2 Natural brown rice-cakes with 1 tbsp honey* | 98 | 0.5 |
| *Strawberries (200g) with 20ml light cream* | 92 | 3.5 |
| *Raspberries (200g) with 20ml light cream* | 82 | 3.5 |
| *100ml low fat plain dairy yoghurt with 15g oat and* | | |
| *honey muesli* | 114 | 2 |
| *Microwave popcorn (100g) and a glass of* | | |
| *orange juice (200ml)* | 98 | 0 |
| *Low sugar jelly (270ml) with pineapple rings in* | | |
| *juice (150g drained)* | 99 | 0 |
| *A glass of skimmed milk (250ml)* | 88 | 0.5 |

Calories  Fat (g)

*Lemon sorbet (50g) with 2 finely chopped almonds*
*sprinkled on top* . . . . . . . . . . . . . . . . . . . . . . . . . . . . . . . .108    4

*Apple Strudel & Custard Twinpot Yoghurt (St Ivel, Shape)* . . . . .56   0.1

*Light & creamy vanilla ice cream (50ml ) with*
*lychees in syrup (50ml drained)* . . . . . . . . . . . . . . . . . . . . . .73    1

## Savoury

*Baby carrots (100g raw, peeled) and 4 x 10cm celery*
*sticks with reduced fat humous (25g, Safeway)* . . . . . . . . .93

*Sugar snap peas (100g) with 1 tbsp taramasalata* . . . . . .104    4

*Iceburg lettuce (35g), cherry tomatoes (100g ),10 slices*
*of cucumber with 2 tbsp French low fat dressing* . . . . . . . .56    0

*1 plain crepe (20g) with 6 Baby Corn (chopped) and*
*1 tbsp cucumber and yoghurt dip* . . . . . . . . . . . . . . . . . . .119   4.5

*Reduced fat mozzarella (30g) with 1 large tomato sliced* . . . . .103   5.5

*1 tbsp low fat cottage cheese and 4 slices of apple*
*on 2 cream crackers* . . . . . . . . . . . . . . . . . . . . . . . . . . . . .78   2.5

*1 slice of rye bread with Philadelphia light*
*medium fat soft cheese (10g, Kraft)* . . . . . . . . . . . . . . . . . .74    2

*1 microwave popadom with 1 tbsp mango chutney* . . . . . .65    0

*5 crab sticks with extra light sour cream (10ml )*
*and 2 tbsp fresh chives* . . . . . . . . . . . . . . . . . . . . . . . . . . .76    1

|  | Calories | Fat (g) |
|---|---|---|
| 1 hard boiled egg (53g) – take out centre and mash with light mayonnaise (Heinz Weight Watchers, 5g) and then spread onto 1 crispbread | 78 | 5.5 |
| Feta Salad – 8 stuffed olives, 5 pieces of sundried tomato in oil (17g drained) and feta cheese (15g) | 106 | 6 |
| Smoked salmon (40g) on 2 Ryvita | 104 | 2 |
| 1 Sainsbury's mini white pitta with raw spinach (35g) and 1 tbsp Italian low fat dressing | 110 | 0.5 |
| 1/2 bagel with 1 tsp marmite and 4 slices of cucumber | 82 | 0.5 |
| 2 sesame crackers with crème fraiche (15ml) and cherry tomatoes (100g halved) | 104 | 8 |
| Cauliflower florets (100g) and broccoli florets (100g) with M&S Mexican Salsa dip (100g) | 78 | 0 |
| Home made potato salad – steamed new potatoes (100g), chopped and mixed with reduced fat mayonnaise (15g) | 117 | 2 |
| Raw beetroot (30g) with Cos lettuce (35g) and 2 oatcakes | 106 | 4 |
| 1 large corn on the cob with Gold Lowest Margarine (10g) | 92 | 4.5 |
| Chicken breast (50g), with no skin and sliced carrots (50g) | 92 | 2.5 |

Calories Fat (g)

## EASY MEALS

### Jacket Potatoes

*Jacket Potato (Medium, 150g) with tuna (50g) and sweetcorn (15g) with reduced fat mayonnaise (5g )* . . . . . . .242   3

*Jacket Potato (Medium, 150g) with 2 tbsp low fat cottage cheese and pineapple* . . . . . . . . . . . . . . . . . . . . .366   1

*Jacket Potato (Medium, 150g) with extra light sour cream (50ml) with 10 slices (90g) of cucumber, and Cos lettuce (70g)* . . . . . . . . . . . . . . . . . . . . . . . . . . . . . . .235   2

*Jacket Potato (Medium, 150g) with chilli con carne (Old El Paso sauce – mince included)* . . . . . . . . . . . . . . .254  6.5

*Jacket Potato (Medium, 150g) with 1/2 tin baked beans (Heinz Weight Watchers)* . . . . . . . . . . . . . . . . . . . . .272  1.4

*Jacket Potato (Medium, 150g) with 2 tbsp low calorie coleslaw* . . . . . . . . . . . . . . . . . . . . . . . . . . . . . .164   3

*Jacket Potato (Medium, 150g) with grated cheddar cheese (30g)* . . . . . . . . . . . . . . . . . . . . . . . . . . . . . . . .258  11

### ...on Toast

*1/2 tin baked beans (Heinz Weight Watchers) on 2 slices of brown toast* . . . . . . . . . . . . . . . . . . . . . . . . . . . . .246   1

*Toasted cheddar cheese (30g) and 1 sliced tomato on 2 slices of brown bread* . . . . . . . . . . . . . . . . . . . . . . .194  11

| | Calories | Fat (g) |
|---|---|---|
| **Ready Meals per serving – (combine with other foods to create 600 calorie meal)** | | |
| *Admiral's Pie (Young's)* | *356* | 16 |
| *Bangers & Cabbage Mash (Safeway Eat Smart)* | *340* | 10 |
| *Beef Lasagne (Tesco organic)* | *389* | 16 |
| *Braised Lamb with carrot & swede mash (Safeway Eat Smart)* | *330* | 10 |
| *Carribbean Spiced Lime & Coconut Chicken with sweet potatoes (M&S Café Culture)* | *510* | 29 |
| *Chicken Breasts with mild & creamy goats cheese (M&S Café Culture)* | *260* | 11 |
| *Chicken Carbonara, Mushrooms & Spinach with Pasta (M&S Steam Cuisine)* | *560* | 28 |
| *Chicken fajitas (Safeway Eat Smart)* | *290* | 4.2 |
| *Chicken korma & rice (Tesco Healthy Eating)* | *483* | 9 |
| *2 Cod Steaks in crispy batter (Birds Eye)* | *480* | 30 |
| *Cod Steak in Parsley Sauce (Birds Eye) per bag boiled* | *150* | 4 |
| *Cottage Pie, vegetarian (Quorn) per 1/2 pack* | *174* | 5 |
| *Greek Style Pastichio (M&S Café Culture)* | *595* | 28 |
| *Haddock Florentine (Safeway Eat Smart)* | *190* | 4.8 |
| *Indian Meal (Tesco Healthy Eating)* | *437* | 9 |
| *Jacket Potato with baked beans & mozzarella cheese (Safeway Eat Smart)* | *225* | 4 |

| | Calories | Fat (g) |
|---|---|---|
| *Jacket Potato with garlic mushrooms & creamy herb sauce (Safeway Eat Smart)* | 225 | 4 |
| *Jacket Potato with chilli con carne (Safeway Eat Smart)* | 225 | 4 |
| *Lemon Chicken (M&S Count on us)* | 420 | 9 |
| *Lasagne, vegetarian (Linda McCartney)* | 374 | 11 |
| *Macaroni Cheese (Safeway Eat Smart)* | 385 | 6.6 |
| *Moussake (M&S Café Culture)* | 525 | 27 |
| *Pork stroganoff with rice (Tesco Healthy Eating)* | 482 | 8 |
| *Quorn tikka masala & rice (Tesco)* | 364 | 10 |
| *Risotto primavera, vegetarian (Safeway Eat Smart)* | 360 | 1.6 |
| *Salmon & broccoli farfalle (Safeway Eat Smart)* | 365 | 9.1 |
| *Salmon en Croute, puff pastry parcels (Tesco) 1 parcel* | 568 | 40 |
| *Seafood Medley, with white wine sauce (M&S Steam Cuisine)* | 320 | 12 |
| *Shepherd's Pie, vegetarian (Linda McCartney)* | 317 | 7 |
| *Steak Chasseur (Tesco Healthy Eating)* | 347 | 8 |
| *2 Spiced Aubergine & Potato Cakes with tomato chutney (M&S Café Culture)* | 490 | 16 |
| *Thai Style Chicken, Noodles, Coconut & Coriander Sauce ( M&S Steam Cuisine)* | 440 | 15 |
| *Tikka Masala & rice, vegetarian (Quorn)* | 476 | 21 |
| *Tomato & Basil Chicken, Fresh Vegetables & Pasta (M&S Steam Cuisine)* | 460 | 14 |

| | Calories | Fat (g) |
|---|---|---|
| *Vegetable Enchiladas (Safeway Eat Smart)* | 305 | 6.7 |
| *Vegetable Stew & Dumplings (Linda McCartney)* | 284 | 11 |

## Lunch Time Ideas – (combine items to create 600 calorie meals)
### Sandwiches per pack

| | Calories | Fat (g) |
|---|---|---|
| *Aromatic Duck (M&S Food to Go)* | 465 | 22 |
| *BLT (Safeway)* | 462 | 28 |
| *Cheese & Celery (M&S Food to Go)* | 465 | 31 |
| *Cheese & Coleslaw (M&S Food to Go)* | 500 | 32 |
| *Cheese & Onion (Safeway)* | 594 | 40 |
| *Cheese & Pickle (Shapers)* | 341 | 8 |
| *Chicken & Bacon (Safeway)* | 400 | 16 |
| *Chicken fajita (Shapers)* | 275 | 5 |
| *Egg Salad (Shapers)* | 304 | 8 |
| *Ham, Cream Cheese & Chive Bagel (Shapers)* | 319 | 7 |
| *Paprika Chicken, Bacon & Tomato (Shapers)* | 297 | 9 |
| *Prawn Mayonnaise (Shapers)* | 320 | 12 |
| *Roast Chicken Salad (Shapers)* | 284 | 6 |
| *Salmon & Cucumber (Shapers)* | 327 | 11 |
| *Spicy Mexican Flatbread (Shapers)* | 297 | 8 |
| *Tuna Sweetcorn (Shapers)* | 317 | 5 |
| *Tuscan Style Tuna Flatbread (Shapers)* | 239 | 2.5 |
| *Wensleydale & Carrot (M&S Food to Go)* | 465 | 31 |

| | Calories | Fat (g) |
|---|---|---|

## Yoghurts per pot

*Apricot Custard Style Yoghurt (Shapers)* . . . . . . . . . . . . . .118  1.1

*Lemon & Lime Yoghurt Mousse (Shapers)* . . . . . . . . . . . . . .89  4

## Salads per pack

*Cheese Layered Salad (Tesco Salad Bowl)* . . . . . . . . . . .592  42

*Pasta, Sundried Tomato & Mozzarella (Tesco Finest)* . . . . .394  24

*Potato Layered Salad (Tesco Salad Bowl)* . . . . . . . . . . . . .284  17

*Pepper, Mushroom & Bacon Pasta Salad*
*(Shape St Ivel) 100g* . . . . . . . . . . . . . . . . . . . . . . . . . . . . .90  3

*Prawn Cocktail Salad (Tesco)* . . . . . . . . . . . . . . . . . . . . . .360  18

*Roast Chicken Salad (Tesco)* . . . . . . . . . . . . . . . . . . . . . . .348  22

*Roasted Red Pepper Pasta Salad (Shape St Ivel) 100g* . . . .92  1

*Sushi Selection (Shapers)* . . . . . . . . . . . . . . . . . . . . . . . . .293  5

*Tabbouleh & Feta Salad (Tesco Finest)* . . . . . . . . . . . . . . .302  11

*Tuna Layered Salad (Tesco Salad Bowl)* . . . . . . . . . . . . . .466  29

## Crisps per bag

*Chargrilled Chicken Flavoured Crinkles (Shapers) 20g bag* . . . .96  5

*Cheese Puffs (Shapers) 16g bag* . . . . . . . . . . . . . . . . . . . . . .83  5

*Doritos, Cool Original Flavour* . . . . . . . . . . . . . . . . . . . . . . .204  10

*Hula Hoops* . . . . . . . . . . . . . . . . . . . . . . . . . . . . . . . . . . . .176  11

*New York Style Pretzels (Shapers) 24g bag* . . . . . . . . . . . . .92  0.6

| | Calories | Fat (g) |
|---|---|---|
| *Salt & Vinegar Sticks (Shapers) 21g bag* . . . . . . . . . . . . . | *95* | 4 |

### Bars per bar

| | | |
|---|---|---|
| *Caramel Bar (Shapers)* . . . . . . . . . . . . . . . . . . . . . . . | *90* | 3 |
| *Cranberry & Apple Bar (Shapers)* . . . . . . . . . . . . . . . . . | *98* | 3 |

### Pasta per 200g cooked serving

| | | |
|---|---|---|
| *Egg* . . . . . . . . . . . . . . . . . . . . . . . . . . . . . . . . . . | *261* | 1 |
| *Plain* . . . . . . . . . . . . . . . . . . . . . . . . . . . . . . . . . | *237* | 0.6 |
| *Ravioli, Cheese and Spinach* . . . . . . . . . . . . . . . . . . | *483* | 13 |
| *Ravolli, Meat* . . . . . . . . . . . . . . . . . . . . . . . . . . . . | *454* | 14 |
| *Tomato & Herb Fettucine* . . . . . . . . . . . . . . . . . . . . | *186* | 1.5 |
| *Tortellini, Cheese and Spinach* . . . . . . . . . . . . . . . . . | *483* | 13 |
| *Wholemeal* . . . . . . . . . . . . . . . . . . . . . . . . . . . . . | *226* | 1.7 |

### Pasta Sauce

| | | |
|---|---|---|
| *Bolognese Sauce (Tesco) 1/2 pot, 175g* . . . . . . . . . . . | *142* | 7 |
| *Carbonara Sauce (Tesco) 1/2 pot, 175g* . . . . . . . . . . . | *289* | 23 |
| *Cheese Sauce (Tesco) 1/2 pot, 175g* . . . . . . . . . . . . . | *184* | 10 |
| *Napoletana Sauce (Tesco) 1/2 pot, 175g* . . . . . . . . . . | *86* | 2.5 |
| *Tomato Dill & Parmesan Sauce (Tesco) 1/2 pot, 175g* . . . . . | *201* | 16 |

### Rice & Noodles per 100g serving

| | | |
|---|---|---|
| *American Brown Rice (Safeway)* . . . . . . . . . . . . . . . . . | *349* | 3 |

| | Calories | Fat (g) |
|---|---|---|
| *American Easy Cook Rice (Safeway)* | 375 | 4 |
| *Basmati Rice (Tesco)* | 347 | 1 |
| *Pilau Rice (Sharwood)* | 354 | 1 |
| *Thai Rice Noodles (Sharwood)* | 361 | 1 |
| *Thick Noodles (Sharwood)* | 340 | 2 |
| *Thread Noodles (Sharwood)* | 340 | 2 |

## Stir Fry

| | Calories | Fat (g) |
|---|---|---|
| *Beansprout Stir Fry (Safeway) per 300g pack* | 165 | 9 |
| *Chicken & Cashew Stir Fry (Tesco) per serving* | 336 | 17 |
| *Chinese Style Chow Mein & Noodles with sauce (Safeway The Best) per 300g pack* | 333 | 13 |
| *Chinese Wok (Findus) per 1/2 pack, 250g* | 113 | 0.5 |
| *Mushroom Stir Fry (Safeway) per 350g pack* | 175 | 9 |
| *Pak Choi Stir Fry (Safeway The Best) per 200g pack* | 170 | 5.7 |
| *Pineapple Stir Fry (Safeway) per 300g pack* | 237 | 15 |
| *Thai Wok (Findus) per 1/2 pack, 250g* | 10 | 0.8 |
| *Vietnamese Wok (Findus) per 1/2 pack, 225g* | 56 | 1.1 |

## Sauces per 100g serving

| | Calories | Fat (g) |
|---|---|---|
| *Black Bean Stir Fry Sauce (Sharwood)* | 93 | 1 |
| *Chilli & Kaffir Lime Leaf Stir Fry Sauce (Sharwood)* | 106 | 6 |
| *Chop Suey Stir Fry Sauce (Sharwood)* | 75 | 2 |

| | Calories | Fat (g) |
|---|---|---|
| *Ginger & Honey Stir Fry Sauce (Sharwood)* . . . . . . . . . . . . .92 | | 0 |
| *Hoi-Sin & Spring Onion Stir Fry Sauce (Sharwood)* . . . . . .133 | | 2 |
| *Lemongrass & Coriander Stir Fry Sauce (Sharwood)* . . . . . .64 | | 2 |
| *Sweet & Sour Stir Fry Sauce (Sharwood)* . . . . . . . . . . . . . .25 | | 0 |
| *Szechuan Stir Fry Sauce (Sharwood)* . . . . . . . . . . . . . . . .21 | | 1 |
| *Teriyaki Stir Fry Sauce (Sharwood)* . . . . . . . . . . . . . . . . . .23 | | 0 |

# EATING IN

On the Slim•Fast Plan, healthy eating is a key element – learning what's good for you is ultimately what is going to keep you on course once you've reached your target.

Please note that manufacturers change the contents of their foods from time to time and this may alter the calorie and fat counts.

www.slimfast.co.uk

| | Calories | Fat (g) |
|---|---|---|

## BISCUITS

### Savoury Biscuits – per biscuit

| | Calories | Fat (g) |
|---|---|---|
| *Dark Rye per slice* | 27 | 0 |
| *Cheddars (McVitie's)* | 543 | 31 |
| *Cheese Melts (Carr's)* | 21 | 1 |
| *Choicegrain Crackers (Jacob's)* | 32 | 1.1 |
| *Crackerbread (Ryvita)* | 383 | 3 |
| *Cream Crackers (Jacob's)* | 35 | 1.1 |
| *Hovis Cracker (Jacob's)* | 27 | 1.1 |
| *Krackawheat (McVitie's)* | 38 | 2 |
| *Matzo Crackers (Rakusen)* | 367 | 2 |
| *Melts (Carr's)* | 19 | 0.9 |
| *Ritz Crackers* | 17 | 1 |
| *Original Ryvita* | 27 | 0 |
| *Sesame Ryvita* | 31 | 1 |
| *Table Water Biscuits, large (Carr's)* | 33 | 0.7 |
| *Table Water Biscuits, small (Carr's)* | 15 | 0.3 |
| *Tuc Biscuits (McVitie's)* | 25 | 1.3 |

### Sweet Biscuits – per biscuit

| | Calories | Fat (g) |
|---|---|---|
| *Abbey Crunch Biscuit (McVitie's)* | 46 | 1.7 |
| *Ace – Milk Chocolate (McVitie's)* | 125 | 5.7 |
| *All Butter Shortbread (McVitie's)* | 77 | 4.2 |

| | Calories | Fat (g) |
|---|---|---|
| *Animal Biscuits* (Cadbury's) 25g | 125 | 5.1 |
| *Blue Riband* (Nestlé) | 109 | 5.6 |
| *BN Chocolate Flavour* | 86 | 3.1 |
| *BN Strawberry Flavour* (McVitie's) | 74 | 1.3 |
| *Boasters – Belgium Chocolate* (McVitie's) | 89 | 5 |
| *Boasters – Hazelnut & Choc Chip* (McVitie's) | 93 | 6 |
| *Butter Puffs* (McVitie's) | 54 | 2.7 |
| *Cafe Noir* (McVitie's) | 39 | 0.5 |
| *Chocolate Digestive Munch Bites* (McVitie's) | 154 | 7.7 |
| *Chocolate Hob Nobs* (McVitie's) | 81 | 3.9 |
| *Chocolate Homewheat* (McVitie's) | 87 | 4.0 |
| *Digestive Creams* (McVitie's) | 63 | 2.9 |
| *Digestive* (McVitie's) | 73 | 3.2 |
| *Fruit Club Biscuits* (Jacob's) | 125 | 6.3 |
| *Fruit Shortcake* (McVitie's) | 39 | 1,6 |
| *Ginger Nut Biscuits* (McVitie's) | 56 | 2 |
| *Gipsy Creams* (McVitie's) | 64 | 3.2 |
| *Hob Nob, original* (McVitie's) | 69 | 3.2 |
| *Iced Gem* (Jacob's) 30g | 116 | 0.9 |
| *Jaffa Cakes* (McVitie's) | 48 | 1 |
| *Light Homewheat Milk Chocolate* (McVitie's) | 79 | 2.9 |
| *Lincoln Biscuits* (McVitie's) | 43 | 2 |
| *Orange Club Biscuits* (Jacob's) | 125 | 7 |

| | Calories | Fat(g) |
|---|---|---|
| Penguin Biscuits (McVitie's) | 131 | 6.8 |
| Plain Chocolate Digestive Caramels (McVitie's) | 83 | 4 |
| Plain Chocolate Ginger Nuts (McVitie's) | 70 | 2.9 |
| Plain Chocolate Hob Nobs (McVitie's) | 96 | 5 |
| Plain Chocolate Hob Nob Tubes (McVitie's) | 96 | 4.7 |
| Plain Chocolate Homewheat (McVitie's) | 88 | 4.2 |
| Rich Tea Biscuits (McVitie's) | 39 | 1.3 |
| Snack Shortcake (Cadbury's) | 220 | 2.7 |

## BREAD per item/ slice

Fat figures are given to the nearest half gram up to three grams
and to the nearest gram thereafter

| | Calories | Fat(g) |
|---|---|---|
| Brown Bread, per slice medium (25g) | 55 | 0.5 |
| Brown Roll, crusty | 140 | 2 |
| Brown Roll, soft | 134 | 2 |
| Crumpet, wholemeal, toasted | 84 | 0.5 |
| Currant Bread, per slice (25g) | 72 | 2 |
| French Stick, 1 white (50g) | 128 | 1.5 |
| Fruit Scone (50g) | 118 | 3 |
| Fruited Teacakes | 180 | 4 |
| Granary Bread, per slice medium (25g) | 59 | 1.0 |
| Granary Roll | 117 | 1 |
| Malt Loaf, 1 slice (35g) | 94 | 0.8 |

| | Calories | Fat (g) |
|---|---|---|
| Naan Bread (160g) | 538 | 20 |
| Pitta Bread, White (95g) | 252 | 1.1 |
| Rye Bread, per slice (25g) | 55 | 0.4 |
| Scone, plain (50g) | 154 | 5 |
| Scotch Pancake | 44 | 2 |
| Wholemeal Bread, per slice medium (25g) | 77 | 1 |
| White Bread, per slice medium (25g) | 59 | 0.5 |
| White Roll, crusty | 140 | 2 |
| White Roll, soft | 134 | 2 |

## CAKES per serving/ slice

| | | |
|---|---|---|
| Almond Slice (Lite & Low) | 69 | 0.8 |
| Apple Bakes (McVitie's Go Ahead) | 128 | 2.8 |
| Bakewell Slices (Mr Kipling) | 151 | 7 |
| Bakewell Tart (Lyons) 1/6 | 142 | 7 |
| Battenburg Cake (Lyons) 230g, 1/6 | 165 | 5.3 |
| Big Bar Caramel Crisp (McVitie's Go Ahead) | 141 | 4 |
| Blueberry Buster Muffin (McVitie's) | 408 | 22 |
| Bounty Cake Bars (McVitie's) | 165 | 9 |
| Bramley Apple Fruit Pie Bars (Mr Kipling) | 170 | 7 |
| Caramel Crisp Bar (McVitie's Go Ahead) | 98 | 3 |
| Caramel Shortbreads (Mr Kipling) | 177 | 10 |
| Cherry & Coconut Flapjacks (Mr Kipling) | 271 | 16 |

| | Calories | Fat (g) |
|---|---|---|
| *Cherry Bakewells* (Mr Kipling) | 190 | 8 |
| *Cherry Genoa Large Slice Cake* (Tesco) 1/8 | 162 | 41 |
| *Choc Caramel Crunch Twinpack* (McVitie's Go Ahead) | 159 | 5 |
| *Choc Chip Cookie* (McVitie's Go Ahead) | 45 | 1.4 |
| *Choc Chip Cake Bar* (McVitie's Go Ahead) | 100 | 4 |
| *Choc Chip Muffin* (McVitie's) | 397 | 21 |
| *Choc Orange Cake Bar* (McVitie's Go Ahead) | 109 | 2 |
| *Choc & Orange Slices* (Lite & Low) | 89 | 0.7 |
| *Chocolate Dream Cake Bar* (McVitie's Go Ahead) | 142 | 5 |
| *Chocolate Bar Cake* (McVitie's) | 384 | 14 |
| *Chocolate Caramel Crunch* (McVitie's Go Ahead) | 106 | 3 |
| *Chocolate Chip Cake* (De Graffe) 1/5 | 332 | 20 |
| *Chocolate Dream Cake Bars* (McVitie's Go Ahead) | 142 | 5 |
| *Chocolate Indulgence Muffin* (McVitie's Go Ahead) | 253 | 7 |
| *Chocolate Muffin* (Cadbury's) | 190 | 12 |
| *Crispy Fruit Slices – Apple & Sultana* (McVitie's Go Ahead) | 58 | 1.2 |
| *Crispy Fruit Slices – Orange & Sultana* (McVitie's Go Ahead) | 60 | 1.2 |
| *Flake Cake Bars* (Cadbury's) | 105 | 5.4 |
| *French Fancies* (Mr Kipling) | 99 | 2.7 |
| *French Sandwich* (Lyons) 1/6 | 142 | 7 |
| *Fruit & Nut Crisp Bar* (McVitie's Go Ahead) | 99 | 3.2 |
| *Galaxy Cake Bar* (McVitie's) | 165 | 9 |
| *Galaxy Caramel Cake Bars* (McVitie's) | 135 | 6 |

| | Calories | Fat (g) |
|---|---|---|
| *Ginger Crisp* (McVitie's Go Ahead) | 26 | 0.6 |
| *Golden Syrup Mini Cakes* (McVitie's) | 126 | 4 |
| *Golden Crunch* (McVitie's Go Ahead) | 36 | 0.8 |
| *Healthy Eating Carrot & Orange Cake Slice* (Tesco) | 80 | 0.8 |
| *Healthy Eating Lemon Cake Slice* (Tesco) | 86 | 0.7 |
| *Homebake Chocolate Cake* (McVitie's) per 100g | 355 | 14 |
| *Homebake Genoa Cake* (McVitie's) per 100g | 383 | 16 |
| *Homebake Lemon Cake* (McVitie's) per 100g | 384 | 18 |
| *Jaffa Cakes Muffin* (McVitie's) | 383 | 18 |
| *Jamaica Ginger Slices* (McVitie's) | 240 | 9 |
| *Lemon Slices* (Mr Kipling) each | 397 | 16 |
| *M & M's Chocolate Brownie* (McVitie's) | 412 | 20 |
| *Manor House Cake* (Mr Kipling) 1/6 | 278 | 14 |
| *Marble Cake* (Tesco) | 212 | 10 |
| *Milk Chocolate Chocolinis* (McVitie's Go Ahead) | 55 | 1.6 |
| *Milky Way Cake Bar* (McVitie's) | 146 | 9 |
| *Mini Battenbergs* (Mr Kipling) | 142 | 3 |
| *Mini Chocolate Cake Bars* (Cadbury's) | 140 | 7 |
| *Mini Chocolate Rolls* (Cadbury's) | 115 | 5 |
| *Mini Classics* (Mr Kipling) | 142 | 7 |
| *Mini Golden Syrup Cake Bar* (McVitie's) | 126 | 4 |
| *Mini Jamaica Ginger Cake Bar* (McVitie's) | 128 | 4 |
| *Mini Juicy Orange Cake Bars* (Cadbury's) | 115 | 5 |

| | Calories | Fat(g) |
|---|---|---|
| *Raspberry & Vanilla Swiss Roll* (Lyons) | 292 | 3 |
| *Real Jam Tarts* (Mr Kipling) | 137 | 5 |
| *Starburst Cake Bar* | 106 | 4 |
| *Strawberry Dream Cake Bar* (McVitie's Go Ahead) | 104 | 1.8 |
| *Strawberry Jam Mini Rolls* (Cadbury's) | 118 | 5 |
| *Strawberry Mallow* (McVitie's Go Ahead) | 79 | 2.3 |
| *Strawberry & Vanilla Swiss Roll* (Tesco) | 118 | 44 |
| *Swiss Gateau* (Cadbury's) 1/6 | 220 | 10 |
| *Toffee Temptation Muffin* (McVitie's Go Ahead) | 297 | 8 |
| *Viennese Whirls* (Mr Kipling) | 138 | 8.4 |

## CEREALS per 30g serving

| | Calories | Fat(g) |
|---|---|---|
| *Advantage* (Weetabix) | 105 | 0.7 |
| *All-Bran* (Kellogg's) | 81 | 1.2 |
| *Alpen* (Weetabix) | 110 | 2.1 |
| *Alpen Caribbean Crunch* (Weetabix) | 121 | 3 |
| *Alpen Nutty Crunch* (Weetabix) | 119 | 3 |
| *Bananabix* (Weetabix) | 111 | 1.5 |
| *Bran Flakes* (Kellogg's) | 96 | 0.9 |
| *Cheerios* (Nestlé) | 111 | 1.1 |
| *Cinnamon Grahams* (Nestlé) | 125 | 3 |
| *Coco Pops* (Kellogg's) | 114 | 0.8 |
| *Coco Shreddies* (Nestlé) | 106 | 0.6 |

| | Calories | Fat(g) |
|---|---|---|
| *Corn Flakes* (Kellogg's) | 111 | 0.3 |
| *Country Store* (Kellogg's) | 108 | 1.5 |
| *Crunchy Nut Cornflakes* (Kellogg's) | 117 | 1.1 |
| *Fibre 1* (Nestlé) | 80 | 0.9 |
| *Force* (Nestlé) | 103 | 0.6 |
| *Frosted Shreddies* (Nestlé) | 107 | 0.3 |
| *Frosties* (Kellogg's) | 114 | 0.2 |
| *Fruit 'n' Fibre* (Kellogg's) | 105 | 1.5 |
| *Golden Grahams* (Nestlé) | 114 | 1.2 |
| *Golden Nuggets* (Nestlé) | 114 | 0.2 |
| *Harvest Crunch* (Quaker) | 138 | 6 |
| *Honey Nut Cheerios* (Nestlé) | 112 | 0.9 |
| *Multi-Grain Start* (Kellogg's) | 108 | 0.6 |
| *Natural Muesli* (Jordan's) | 106 | 2.1 |
| *Nesquick* (Nestlé) | 119 | 1.5 |
| *Perfect Balance* (Heinz Weight Watchers) | 90 | 0.6 |
| *Porridge, made with wholemilk* | 35 | 1.5 |
| *Porridge, made with water* | 15 | 0.3 |
| *Quaker Puffed Wheat* (Quaker) | 98 | 0.3 |
| *Ready Brek* (Weetabix) | 107 | 2.4 |
| *Ready Brek Chocolate* (Weetabix) | 108 | 2.1 |
| *Rice Krispies* (Kellogg's) | 111 | 0.3 |
| *Ricicles* (Kellogg's) | 114 | 0.3 |

| | Calories | Fat (g) |
|---|---|---|
| *Shredded Wheat* | 99 | 0.6 |
| *Shreddies* | 103 | 0.6 |
| *Special K (Kellogg's)* | 111 | 0.3 |
| *Sugar Puffs (Quaker)* | 116 | 0.3 |
| *Sultana Bran (Kellogg's)* | 96 | 0.6 |
| *Weetabix (Weetabix)* | 102 | 0.9 |
| *Weetos (Weetabix)* | 115 | 1.5 |

## CONFECTIONERY per standard bar

| | Calories | Fat (g) |
|---|---|---|
| *Aero (Nestlé)* | 199 | 11 |
| *Aero Honeycomb (Nestlé)* | 199 | 10 |
| *Aero Creamy White Centre (Nestlé)* | 257 | 15 |
| *After Eight Mints (Nestlé) per 100g* | 419 | 13 |
| *Black Magic Assortment (Nestlé) per 100g* | 453 | 21 |
| *Boost (Cadbury's)* | 295 | 16 |
| *Bounty Milk Chocolate (Mars)* | 276 | 15 |
| *Bournville Chocolate (Cadbury's)* | 225 | 12 |
| *California Dream (Cadbury's)* | 250 | 15 |
| *Caramel (Cadbury's)* | 240 | 12 |
| *Chocolate Buttons (Cadbury's) 65g pack* | 340 | 19 |
| *Chocolate Cream (Fry's)* | 215 | 8 |
| *Chocolate Orange (Terry's)* | 445 | 26 |
| *Chocolate Tracker (Mars)* | 188 | 10 |

| | Calories | Fat(g) |
|---|---|---|
| *Crunchie (Cadbury's)* | 470 | 18 |
| *Curly Wurly (Cadbury's)* | 130 | 5 |
| *Dairy Box Assortment (Nestlé) per 100g* | 471 | 22 |
| *Dairy Milk Chocolate (Cadbury's) 6 pieces* | 260 | 15 |
| *Dairy Milk Tasters (Cadbury) per bag* | 255 | 13 |
| *Dime (Kraft)* | 155 | 10 |
| *Double Decker (Cadbury's)* | 300 | 14 |
| *Drifter (Nestlé)* | 296 | 14 |
| *Flake (Cadbury's)* | 360 | 20 |
| *Flyte (Mars)* | 98 | 3.2 |
| *Fox's – Fruits (Nestlé) per 100g* | 386 | 0 |
| *Fox's Glacier Mints (Nestlé) per 100g* | 386 | 0 |
| *Fruit & Nut Chocolate (Cadbury's)* | 240 | 13 |
| *Fruit & Nut Tasters (Cadbury's) per bag* | 230 | 13 |
| *Fruit Gums (Rowntree) per 12 sweets* | 164 | 0.1 |
| *Fruit Pastilles (Rowntree) per 12 sweets* | 184 | 0 |
| *Fudge (Cadbury's)* | 115 | 4.2 |
| *Fuse (Cadbury's)* | 240 | 12 |
| *Galaxy Caramel (Mars) twin bar* | 233 | 12 |
| *Galaxy Milk Chocolate (Mars)* | 540 | 32 |
| *Heroes (Cadbury's) per 100g* | 490 | 26 |
| *Jellytots (Nestlé) per 100g* | 346 | 0 |
| *Kit Kat (Nestlé)* | 247 | 13 |

| | Calories | Fat (g) |
|---|---|---|
| *Lion Bar* (Nestlé) | 269 | 12 |
| *Maltesers* (Mars) 40.7g pack | 197 | 9.3 |
| *Marble* (Cadbury's) | 265 | 14.4 |
| *Mars Bar* (Mars) | 281 | 11 |
| *Milk Chocolate Aero* (Nestlé) | 200 | 11 |
| *Milk Chocolate Yorkie* (Nestlé) | 370 | 21 |
| *Milk Tray* (Cadbury's) per 100g | 495 | 26 |
| *Milky Way* (Mars) 26g bar | 117 | 4.3 |
| *Mint Chocolate Aero* (Nestlé) | 254 | 14 |
| *Mint Matchmakers* (Nestlé) 1/2 pack, 72g | 343 | 14 |
| *Munchies* (Nestlé) | 255 | 12 |
| *Nuts about Caramel* (Cadbury's) | 275 | 15 |
| *Old Jamaica* (Cadbury's) per 100g | 465 | 23 |
| *Orange Cream* (Cadbury's) | 257 | 15 |
| *Peppermint Cream* (Fry's) | 215 | 8 |
| *Picnic* (Cadbury's) | 230 | 11 |
| *Polo – Fruits* (Nestlé) per 100g | 384 | 0 |
| *Polo – Spearmint* (Nestlé) per 100g | 402 | 1 |
| *Polo – Sugar Free* (Nestlé) 100g pack | 238 | 0 |
| *Polo – Supermint* (Nestlé) per 100g | 393 | 1 |
| *Quality Street* (Nestlé) per 100g | 466 | 21 |
| *Revels* (Mars) per pack | 172 | 8 |
| *Rolo* (Nestlé) 1 tube | 273 | 12 |

| | Calories | Fat(g) |
|---|---|---|
| *Roses (Cadbury's) per 100g* | 485 | 25 |
| *Smarties (Nestlé) per 100g* | 459 | 16 |
| *Snickers (Mars)* | 322 | 18 |
| *Snow Flake (Cadbury's)* | 200 | 11 |
| *Star Burst Flipsters (Mars) 10 sweets* | 145 | 0 |
| *Tic Tac per 100g* | 386 | 0 |
| *Time Out (Cadbury's)* | 190 | 11 |
| *Toffee Crisp (Nestlé)* | 243 | 13 |
| *Topic (Mars)* | 231 | 12 |
| *Turkish Delight (Fry's)* | 185 | 4 |
| *Twirl (Cadbury's)* | 230 | 14 |
| *Twix (Mars)* | 287 | 14 |
| *Fudge (Cadbury's)* | 115 | 4.2 |
| *Walnut Whip (Nestlé)* | 165 | 8.4 |
| *Wholenut Chocolate (Cadbury's)* | 270 | 17 |
| *Wholenut Tasters (Cadbury's) per bag* | 250 | 17 |
| *Wispa (Cadbury's)* | 215 | 13 |
| *Wispa Bite (Cadbury's)* | 240 | 13 |
| *Wispa Gold (Cadbury's)* | 265 | 15 |
| *Wispa Mint (Cadbury's)* | 275 | 17 |
| *Yorkie (Nestlé)* | 370 | 21 |

| | Calories | Fat (g) |
|---|---|---|

## CHILLED READY MEALS

### Asda Good For You per serving

| | Calories | Fat (g) |
|---|---|---|
| Chicken & Pasta | 296 | 12 |
| Chicken Arrabiatta | 227 | 4 |
| Chicken Korma & Pilau Rice | 600 | 24 |
| Chicken Tikka Massala & Pilau Rice | 594 | 18 |
| Liver, Bacon & Mash | 455 | 15 |
| Mushroom & Tomato Tagliatelle | 213 | 5 |
| Spinach & Ricotta Cannelloni | 418 | 10 |
| Sweet & Sour Chicken & Egg Fried Rice | 581 | 13 |

### Asda per serving

| | Calories | Fat (g) |
|---|---|---|
| American Chicken & Black Bean Chilli with Rice | 799 | 35 |
| Quorn Fillets in a Lemon & Black Pepper Sauce | 189 | 9 |
| Quorn Lasagne | 249 | 9 |
| Quorn Spaghetti Bolognese | 275 | 5 |
| Bangers & Mash | 505 | 25 |
| Beef & Ale Stew with Dumplings | 526 | 26 |
| Broccoli Mornay | 217 | 13 |
| Cheese & Onion Mash, 1 pack | 384 | 9 |
| Chicken, Bacon & Mushroom Bake | 592 | 32 |
| Chicken & Blackbean with Egg Fried Rice | 737 | 21 |

| | Calories | Fat(g) |
|---|---|---|
| *Chicken & Cashew Nut with Egg Fried Rice* | 706 | 30 |
| *Chicken Enchiladas* | 420 | 12 |
| *Chicken Fajita* | 755 | 31 |
| *Chicken Jalfrezi,1 pack* | 415 | 20 |
| *Chicken Korma with Pilau Rice* | 803 | 35 |
| *Chicken Korma,1 pack* | 714 | 48 |
| *Chicken Madras & Pilau Rice* | 588 | 28 |
| *Chicken Madras* | 418 | 31 |
| *Chicken Tandoori Masala & Pilau Rice* | 597 | 21 |
| *Chicken Tikka Masala & Pilau Rice* | 584 | 20 |
| *Chicken Tikka Masala* | 343 | 17 |
| *Chicken Turkey Satay, 6 sticks* | 259 | 17 |
| *Chilli Beef & Nachos* | 357 | 21 |
| *Corned Beef Hash with a Fresh Potato Topping* | 367 | 3 |
| *Cottage Pie* | 360 | 16 |
| *Cumberland Pie* | 358 | 14 |
| *Lasagne* | 445 | 25 |
| *Leek & Bacon Pasta Bake* | 626 | 46 |
| *Macaroni Cheese* | 423 | 27 |
| *Mushroom Dopiac, 1 pack* | 265 | 14 |
| *Red Thai Style Curry with Rice* | 597 | 11 |
| *Shepherds Pie* | 390 | 22 |
| *Spaghetti Bolognese* | 262 | 10 |

| | Calories | Fat (g) |
|---|---|---|
| *Steak & Mushroom Potato Topped Pie* | 356 | 16 |
| *Sweet & Sour Chicken with Egg Fried Rice* | 761 | 25 |
| *Tandoori Chicken Masala with Pilau Rice* | 597 | 21 |
| *Tuna Al Forno* | 443 | 19 |
| *Vegetarian Fajitas* | 417 | 21 |
| *Vegetable Pasta Bake* | 226 | 10 |
| *Vegetable Lasagne* | 474 | 22 |

### Birds Eye Ready Meals per portion/ piece

| | Calories | Fat (g) |
|---|---|---|
| *Beef Curry with Rice (Birds Eye)* | 506 | 11 |
| *Beef Lasagne (Birds Eye)* | 503 | 23 |
| *Beef Stew & Dumplings (Birds Eye)* | 336 | 13 |
| *Chicken Breast in Gravy (Birds Eye) per pack* | 125 | 1.6 |
| *Chicken Curry with Rice (Birds Eye)* | 469 | 8 |
| *Chicken Jalfrezi (Birds Eye) per pack* | 455 | 37 |
| *Chicken Lattice – Bacon & Cheese (Birds Eye)* | 398 | 25 |
| *Chicken Lattice – Cheese & Broccoli (Birds Eye)* | 392 | 23 |
| *Chicken Lattice – Creamy Mushroom (Birds Eye)* | 389 | 23 |
| *Chicken Pies (Birds Eye)* | 471 | 28 |
| *Chicken Stew & Dumplings (Birds Eye)* | 352 | 16 |
| *Chicken Supreme with Rice (Birds Eye)* | 480 | 11 |
| *Chicken Tikka Masala with Pilau Rice (Birds Eye)* | 506 | 15 |
| *Chilli Con Carne (Birds Eye)* | 308 | 6 |

| | Calories | Fat (g) |
|---|---|---|
| *Italiano Bake* (Birds Eye) 1 piece | 176 | 6 |
| *Lamb Curry with Rice* (Birds Eye) | 476 | 11 |
| *Lean Roast Beef & Gravy* (Birds Eye) 114g | 111 | 5 |
| *Lemon Pepper Chicken* (Birds Eye) 1 piece | 242 | 12 |
| *Macaroni Cheese* (Birds Eye) | 353 | 14 |
| *Minced Beef & Onion Pies* (Birds Eye) 1 pie | 448 | 26 |
| *Prawn Curry with Rice* (Birds Eye) | 443 | 8 |
| *Roast Beef Dinner* (Birds Eye) | 357 | 11 |
| *Roast Chicken Dinner* (Birds Eye) | 364 | 11 |
| *Roast Lamb Dinner* (Birds Eye) | 337 | 10 |
| *Roast Pork Dinner* (Birds Eye) | 320 | 7 |
| *Roast Turkey Dinner* (Birds Eye) | 313 | 10 |
| *Shepherds Pie* (Birds Eye) 227g | 229 | 11 |
| *Southern Fried Chicken* (Birds Eye) 1 piece | 278 | 18 |
| *Spaghetti Bolognese* (Birds Eye) | 380 | 14 |
| *Spicy Mexican Chicken* (Birds Eye) 1 piece | 247 | 14 |
| *Steak & Kidney Pies* (Birds Eye) | 367 | 28 |
| *Thai Chicken* (Birds Eye) | 213 | 15 |

## Marks & Spencer Count on Us per serving

| | | |
|---|---|---|
| *Chicken Tikka Masala* | 293 | 8 |
| *Ham Tagliatelle* | 360 | 9 |
| *Lasagne* | 325 | 8 |

| | Calories | Fat (g) |
|---|---|---|
| Spaghetti Bolognese | 360 | 6 |

### Marks & Spencer per serving

| | Calories | Fat (g) |
|---|---|---|
| Bangers & Mash | 480 | 29 |
| Beef Casserole | 260 | 10 |
| Cannelloni | 540 | 33 |
| Chicken Balti | 375 | 23 |
| Chicken Jalfrezi | 450 | 30 |
| Chicken Korma | 525 | 30 |
| Chicken Piri Piri | 420 | 23 |
| Chicken Risotto | 415 | 15 |
| Chicken Sag | 420 | 27 |
| Chicken Spiralli | 398 | 15 |
| Chicken Tikka Masala | 585 | 41 |
| Cod Bake & Spinach | 670 | 42 |
| Cottage Pie | 240 | 13 |
| Haddock & Cheese Mornay | 440 | 23 |
| Ham Tagliatelle | 415 | 41 |
| Lamb Rogan Josh | 360 | 15 |
| Lasagne | 595 | 30 |
| Macaroni Cheese | 540 | 30 |
| Moussaka "Cafe Culture" 1/2 pack | 525 | 27 |
| Mushroom Risotto | 418 | 16 |

| | Calories | Fat (g) |
|---|---|---|
| *Prawn Rogan Josh* | 465 | 35 |
| *Roast Beef Meal* | 460 | 24 |
| *Roast Duck à l'Orange* | 1110 | 84 |
| *Roast Lamb Meal* | 460 | 19 |
| *Salmon & Prawn Bake* | 830 | 56 |
| *Scottish Salmon en Croute* | 1110 | 78 |
| *Shepherds Pie* | 210 | 9 |
| *Spaghetti Bolognese* | 575 | 29 |
| *Thai Prawn Green Curry* | 610 | 28 |
| *Vegetable Curry* | 435 | 36 |

### Safeway Eat Smart per serving

| | Calories | Fat (g) |
|---|---|---|
| *Eat Smart Bangers & Cabbage Mash* | 340 | 10 |
| *Eat Smart Braised Lamb with Carrot & Swede Mash* | 330 | 10 |
| *Eat Smart Cauliflower Cheese* | 160 | 6 |
| *Eat Smart Chicken Fajitas* | 290 | 4 |
| *Eat Smart Chicken Tikka Masala and rice* | 280 | 5 |
| *Eat Smart Haddock Florentine* | 190 | 5 |
| *Eat Smart Jacket Potato with Baked Beans & Mozzarella* | 225 | 4 |
| *Eat Smart Jacket Potato with Chilli con Carne* | 225 | 4 |
| *Eat Smart Jacket Potato with Garlic Mushrooms & Creamy Herb Sauce* | 210 | 8 |
| *Eat Smart Lasagne* | 360 | 10 |

| | Calories | Fat (g) |
|---|---|---|
| *Eat Smart Macaroni Cheese* | 385 | 7 |
| *Eat Smart Risotto Primavera, Vegetarian* | 360 | 2 |
| *Eat Smart Salmon & Broccoli Farfalle* | 365 | 9 |
| *Eat Smart Vegetable Enchiladas* | 305 | 7 |

### Safeway per serving

| | | |
|---|---|---|
| *Balti Chicken Curry & Naan Bread* | 760 | 33 |
| *Basmati Rice* | 509 | 17 |
| *Beef Lasagne* | 504 | 22 |
| *Beef Stew & Dumplings* | 536 | 26 |
| *Beef Stroganoff* | 399 | 27 |
| *Bengali Vegetable Curry* | 178 | 8 |
| *Bombay Potato* | 144 | 4 |
| *Broccoli & Mushroom Filled Yorkshire Pudding* | 372 | 22 |
| *Broccoli Mornay* | 203 | 13 |
| *Butter Chicken* | 689 | 50 |
| *Cannelloni* | 482 | 23 |
| *Cauliflower Cheese* | 496 | 35 |
| *Cauliflower, Broccoli & Carrot Gruyère Bake* | 462 | 31 |
| *Chicken & Broccoli Cumberland Pie* | 280 | 10 |
| *Chicken & Broccoli Pasta Bake* | 487 | 21 |
| *Chicken Biryani & Vegetable Curry* | 571 | 23 |
| *Chicken Stew with Dumplings* | 684 | 42 |

| | Calories | Fat (g) |
|---|---|---|
| Chicken Chow Mein and Fresh Vegetables | 368 | 13 |
| Chicken Fajitas | 340 | 10 |
| Chicken Jalfrezi | 474 | 20 |
| Chicken Korma | 648 | 39 |
| Chicken Korma & Rice | 1020 | 37 |
| Chicken Lasagne | 852 | 38 |
| Chicken Madras | 469 | 25 |
| Chicken Pasanda | 686 | 45 |
| Chicken Piri Piri | 578 | 31 |
| Chicken Risotto | 452 | 11 |
| Chicken Saag | 504 | 29 |
| Chicken Tikka Masala | 487 | 22 |
| Chicken Vindaloo | 448 | 22 |
| Chilli Con Carne | 430 | 2.6 |
| Cottage Pie | 431 | 16 |
| Fish Pie | 428 | 18 |
| Ham & Mushroom Tagliatelle | 664 | 44 |
| Lamb Rogan Josh | 630 | 39 |
| Lancashire Hot Pot | 312 | 10 |
| Liver & Bacon with Mash | 508 | 23 |
| Luxury Beef Lasagne | 864 | 46 |
| Luxury Cumberland Fish Pie | 428 | 18 |
| Luxury Roasted Vegetable Lasagne | 492 | 20 |

| | Calories | Fat (g) |
|---|---|---|
| *Mushroom Risotto* | 434 | 12 |
| *Penne Mozzarella* | 588 | 19 |
| *Penne Nicoise* | 500 | 24 |
| *Pilau Rice* | 492 | 16 |
| *Rigatoni Bolognese Bake* | 529 | 25 |
| *Roast Beef & Veg Filled Yorkshire Pudding* | 662 | 33 |
| *Seafood Linguine* | 369 | 28 |
| *Spaghetti Bolognese* | 288 | 5 |
| *Spaghetti Carbonara* | 588 | 40 |
| *Spinach & Ricotta Cannelloni* | 396 | 19 |
| *Sweet & Sour Pork* | 503 | 15 |
| *Tuna Pasta Bake* | 507 | 22 |
| *Vegetable Chilli* | 196 | 4 |
| *Vegetable Fajitas* | 189 | 9 |
| *Vegetable Lasagne* | 342 | 13 |
| *Vegetable Cumberland Pie* | 342 | 18 |

### Sainsbury's Be Good To Yourself per serving

#### BGTY – Be Good To Youself 95% Fat Free

| | | |
|---|---|---|
| BGTY Braised Beef Casserole | 410 | 9 |
| BGTY Cauliflower Cheese | 472 | 14 |
| BGTY Chicken Amatriciana with Tagliatelle | 482 | 15 |
| BGTY Caribbean Fruity Chicken with Rice & Peas | 509 | 15 |

| | Calories | Fat(g) |
|---|---|---|
| BGTY Chicken & Blackbean Sauce with Egg Fried Rice | 567 | 23 |
| BGTY Chicken Casserole | 100 | 4 |
| BGTY Chicken Chow Mein | 423 | 13.5 |
| BGTY Chicken Jalfrezi & Pilau Rice | 432 | 4.5 |
| BGTY Chicken Korma with Pilau Rice | 511 | 9 |
| BGTY Chicken Tikka Makhani with Pilau Rice | 428 | 4.5 |
| BGTY Chicken Tikka Masala with Pilau Rice | 514 | 5.9 |
| BGTY Chicken & Asparagus | 504 | 4.5 |
| BGTY Chicken, Broccoli & Mushroom Pie | 423 | 9 |
| BGTY Gnocco Sardo with Chicken & Primavera Sauce | 558 | 9 |
| BGTY Fat Free Lasagne | 500 | 18 |
| BGTY Mango Chicken & Rice | 571 | 6.8 |
| BGTY Fat Free Macaroni Cheese | 549 | 9 |
| BGTY Pork in Mustard Sauce with Colcannon Mash | 369 | 9 |
| BGTY Roast Vegetable & Spirali Pasta | 423 | 18 |
| BGTY Salmon & Spinach Cannelloni | 522 | 21 |
| BGTY Shepherds Pie | 441 | 13.5 |
| BGTY Spaghetti Bolognese | 392 | 4.5 |
| BGTY Sweet & Sour Chicken & Egg Fried Rice | 675 | 18 |
| BGTY Tagliatelle With Ham & Mushroom | 495 | 18 |

### Sainsbury's per serving

| | Calories | Fat(g) |
|---|---|---|
| Cantonese Sweet & Sour Chicken in a Crispy Batter | 610 | 27 |

| | Calories | Fat (g) |
|---|---|---|
| Cantonese Sweet & Sour Pork | 199 | 7 |
| Classic British Chicken Casserole with Dumplings | 612 | 32 |
| Classic British Lancashire Hot Pot | 439 | 14 |
| Classic British Liver & Bacon in Onion Gravy | 572 | 27 |
| Classic British Minced Beef Hot Pot | 557 | 5 |
| Classic British Roast Beef Meal | 442 | 14 |
| Classic British Roast Chicken Meal | 458 | 12 |
| Classic British Sausage Yorkshire Pudding | 862 | 44 |
| Classic British Shepherd's Pie | 505 | 23 |
| Corned Beef Hash | 481 | 24 |
| Cottage Pie | 295 | 15 |
| Fishermans Pie | 311 | 12 |
| Fresh Cauliflower Cheese | 245 | 32 |
| Fresh Colcannon Mashed Potato | 559 | 32 |
| Indian Aloo Saag Curry | 119 | 12 |
| Indian Aubergine Masala Curry | 234 | 13 |
| Indian Bombay Potato Curry | 132 | 10 |
| Indian Channa Masala Curry | 176 | 8 |
| Indian Chicken Madras Curry | 317 | 44 |
| Indian Chicken Saag Masala Curry | 283 | 14 |
| Indian Chicken Tikka Biryani Curry | 349 | 27 |
| Indian Chicken Tikka Masala Curry | 368 | 26 |
| Indian Chicken Vindaloo Curry | 293 | 18 |

| | Calories | Fat (g) |
|---|---|---|
| Indian Creamy Prawn Masala Curry & Rice | 749 | 14 |
| Indian Daal Curry | 132 | 8 |
| Indian Lamb Rogan Josh Curry | 329 | 22 |
| Indian Pilau Rice | 333 | 4 |
| Indian Tamarind Chicken Curry | 273 | 16 |
| Indian Tandoori Chicken Sizzler Curry | 268 | 14 |
| Indian Vegetable Biryani Curry | 295 | 16 |
| Indian Vegetable Curry | 156 | 10 |
| Italian Chicken & Bacon Risotto | 614 | 27 |
| Italian Chicken Lasagne | 557 | 23 |
| Italian Five Cheese Tortelloni | 356 | 23 |
| Italian Lamb Ragu Al Forno | 632 | 23 |
| Italian Lasagne | 652 | 32 |
| Italian Mushroom Cannelloni | 665 | 36 |
| Italian Penne Nicoise | 402 | 14 |
| Italian Penne with Leeks & Bacon | 756 | 32 |
| Italian Pork Meatballs Al Forno | 641 | 23 |
| Italian Roasted Vegetable Lasagne | 726 | 41 |
| Italian Roasted Vegetable Lasagnetti | 495 | 18 |
| Italian Six Cheese Al Forno | 747 | 32 |
| Italian Spaghetti Bolognese | 579 | 23 |
| Italian Spaghetti Carbonara | 684 | 45 |
| Italian Spinach & Cheese Lasagne | 617 | 36 |

| | Calories | Fat(g) |
|---|---|---|
| *Italian Spinach & Ricotta Cannelloni* | 729 | 41 |
| *Italian Spirali & Pepperoni* | 609 | 27 |
| *Italian Tomato & Cheese Al Forno* | 612 | 23 |
| *Italian Tuna & Sweetcorn Pasta* | 712 | 14 |
| *Italian Tuscan Chicken* | 206 | 14 |
| *Lasagne* | 433 | 18 |
| *Macaroni Cheese* | 319 | 13 |
| *Macaroni & Bolognese Bake* | 372 | 12 |
| *Mediterranean Moussaka* | 653 | 36 |
| *Moghlai Butter Chicken Curry* | 290 | 23 |
| *Moghlai Chicken Korma Curry* | 290 | 16 |
| *Moghlai Chicken Korma & Rice* | 324 | 16 |
| *Moghlai Chicken Lababdar Curry* | 279 | 27 |
| *Moghlai Chicken Makhani Curry with Pilau Rice* | 300 | 14 |
| *Moghlai Chicken Pasanda Curry* | 331 | 22 |
| *Moghlai Lamb Biryani Curry* | 390 | 16 |
| *Penne Tomato & Tuna* | 585 | 15 |
| *Potato Gratin* | 373 | 27 |
| *Potato, Cheese & Onion Bake* | 350 | 16 |
| *Quorn Casserole with Herb Dumplings* | 562 | 27 |
| *Quorn Cottage Pie* | 327 | 9 |
| *Quorn Korma & Pilau Rice* | 716 | 23 |
| *Spaghetti Bolognese* | 401 | 9 |

| | Calories | Fat(g) |
|---|---|---|
| Spaghetti Tomato & Cheese | 561 | 15 |
| Thai Yellow Vegetable Curry | 649 | 12 |
| Vegetable Lasagne | 344 | 12 |

## Tesco Healthy Eating per serving

| | | |
|---|---|---|
| Beef Cannelloni | 360 | 6 |
| Sweet Chilli Chicken | 392 | 1.2 |
| Cauliflower Cheese | 164 | 6 |
| Chicken, Vegetable & Pasta Bake | 344 | 7 |
| Chicken Tikka Masala | 472 | 11 |
| Cottage Pie | 348 | 9 |
| Fisherman's Pie | 308 | 2 |
| Pork, Chicken & Broccoli | 312 | 6 |

## Tesco per serving

| | | |
|---|---|---|
| Bangers & Mash | 492 | 23 |
| Beef Stew & Dumplings | 424 | 18 |
| Broccoli in Cheese & Tomato Sauce | 225 | 12 |
| Cauliflower Cheese | 207 | 10 |
| Chicken & Bacon Pasta Bake | 464 | 14 |
| Chicken Balti with Rice | 265 | 6 |
| Chicken Jalfrezi with Rice | 469 | 14 |
| Chicken Korma | 764 | 44 |

| | Calories | Fat (g) |
|---|---|---|
| Chicken Madras with Rice | 515 | 20 |
| Chicken Tikka Masala | 460 | 44 |
| Chinese Chicken, Mushrooms & Egg Fried Rice | 474 | 13 |
| "Finest" Beef Casserole & Ale with Rice | 222 | 3.2 |
| Lancashire Hot Pot | 412 | 14 |
| Lasagne | 390 | 15 |
| Liver & Bacon Hot Pot | 468 | 17 |
| Macaroni Cheese | 576 | 26 |
| Beef & Vegetable Yorkshire | 390 | 15 |
| Shepherds Pie | 238 | 8 |
| Spaghetti Bolognese | 356 | 7 |
| Cheese & Tomato Bake | 388 | 6 |
| Sweet & Sour Chicken | 478 | 12 |
| Thai Green Curry | 616 | 28 |
| Vegetable Hot Pot | 326 | 16 |

## Waitrose per serving

| | Calories | Fat (g) |
|---|---|---|
| Beef Stew & Dumplings | 549 | 22 |
| Chicken Casserole | 428 | 21 |
| Chicken Korma | 631 | 43 |
| Chicken Tikka Makhani | 450 | 28 |
| Chilli Con Carne & Rice | 468 | 12 |
| Cottage Pie | 337 | 12 |

| | Calories | Fat(g) |
|---|---|---|
| *Cumberland Pie* | *128* | *6* |
| *Cod & Salmon Lasagne* | *434* | *17* |
| *Green Chutney Chicken* | *487* | *25* |
| *Ham & Mushroom Tagliatelle* | *580* | *31* |
| *Duck with Plum Sauce* | *187* | *12* |
| *Lamb Hot Pot* | *416* | *9* |
| *Lasagne* | *469* | *22* |
| *Lemon Chicken* | *488* | *18* |
| *Moussaka* | *507* | *29* |
| *Mushroom Risotto* | *277* | *17* |
| *Red Thai Chicken Curry* | *489* | *32* |
| *Salmon & Prawn Tagliatelle* | *85* | *3* |
| *Shepherds Pie* | *413* | *20* |
| *Spaghetti Bolognese* | *483* | *20* |
| *Steak & Mushroom Pie* | *488* | *29* |
| *Sweet & Sour Pork (300g pack)* | *324* | *10* |
| *Tandoori Bhuna Chicken* | *534* | *35* |
| *Thai Green Chicken Curry* | *308* | *16* |
| *Tuna & Pasta Bake* | *536* | *20* |
| *Vegetable Lasagne* | *447* | *32* |
| *Vegetable Moussaka* | *529* | *34* |
| *Vegetable Fusilli Bake* | *151* | *10* |

## COOKING SAUCES per 100g

|  | Calories | Fat (g) |
|---|---|---|
| Balti Cook-in-Sauce (Homepride) | 68 | 3 |
| Balti Stir & Sizzle Duo Jar (Chicken Tonight) | 103 | 8 |
| Barbecue Cook-in-Sauce (Homepride) | 83 | 2 |
| Basil & Oregano (RAGU) | 38 | 0 |
| Bolognese Sauce (Tesco) | 81 | 4 |
| Cape Malay Curry New World Sauce (Knorr) | 114 | 4 |
| Carbonara Pasta Sauce (Tesco) | 165 | 13 |
| Char-Grilled Summer Vegetables (Bertolli) | 60 | 2 |
| Chasseur Cook-in-Sauce (Homepride) | 40 | 0 |
| Cheese Sauce Classic Sauce Mix (Knorr) | 469 | 32 |
| Cheese & Bacon Potato Bake (Homepride) | 132 | 13 |
| Cheese & Onion Potato Bake (Homepride) | 141 | 12 |
| Creamy Tikka Sauce (Chicken Tonight) | 128 | 8 |
| Chicken & Mushroom Potato Bake (Homepride) | 122 | 12 |
| Chilli Cook-in-Sauce (Homepride) | 60 | 1 |
| Chunky Onions & Garlic (RAGU) | 65 | 1 |
| Coronation Sauce (Heinz) | 334 | 31 |
| Country French Sauce (Chicken Tonight) | 94 | 8 |
| Creamy Curry Sauce (Chicken Tonight) | 85 | 7 |
| Creamy Ham Pour Over Sauce (Knorr) | 81 | 75 |
| Creamy Ham & Mushroom Pasta Stir & Serve Sauce (Homepride) | 135 | 12 |
| Creamy Mushroom Sauce (Chicken Tonight) | 87 | 7 |

|  | Calories | Fat (g) |
|---|---|---|
| *Creamy Peppercorn Sauce* (Chicken Tonight) | 80 | 7 |
| *Curry Sauce Cook-in-Sauce* (Homepride) | 108 | 8 |
| *Deliciously Good Korma Curry Sauce* (Homepride) | 88 | 4 |
| *Deliciously Good Mexican Chilli – Hot* (Homepride) | 52 | 1 |
| *Deliciously Good Mexican Chilli – Medium* (Homepride) | 56 | 1 |
| *Deliciously Good Mushroom & Garlic Cook-in-Sauce* (Homepride) | 74 | 5 |
| *Deliciously Good Rogan Josh Curry Sauce* (Homepride) | 60 | 1 |
| *Deliciously Good Tikka Masala Curry Sauce* (Homepride) | 81 | 4 |
| *Fajita Stir Fry Sauce Stir It Up* (Chicken Tonight) | 589 | 54 |
| *Flamegrill Texas Hot American BBQ Style Sauce* (Heinz) | 123 | 0 |
| *Franshoek Fruity Curry New World Sauce* (Knorr) | 81 | 3 |
| *Garlic & Herb Potato Bake* (Homepride) | 153 | 15 |
| *Hawaiian Sweet & Sour American BBQ Style Sauce* (Heinz) | 127 | 2 |
| *Hearty Cumberland Sausage* (Colman's) | 34 | 0 |
| *Hollandaise Pour Over Sauce* (Knorr) | 79 | 7 |
| *Hollandaise Sauce Bonne Cuisine Sauce* (Crosse & Blackwell) | 390 | 17 |
| *Honey & Mustard Sauce* (Chicken Tonight) | 106 | 5 |
| *Jalfrezi Stir & Sizzle Duo Jar* (Chicken Tonight) | 113 | 10 |
| *Jamaican Jerk Stir Fry Sauce Stir It Up* (Chicken Tonight) | 625 | 58 |
| *Japanese Teryaki Stir Fry Sauce Stir It Up* (Chicken Tonight) | 611 | 8 |
| *Karoo Tomato Bredie New World Sauce* (Knorr) | 31 | 0 |
| *Korma Curry Cook-in-Sauce* (Homepride) | 68 | 2 |
| *Korma Stir & Sizzle Duo Jar* (Chicken Tonight) | 241 | 21 |

| | Calories | Fat(g) |
|---|---|---|
| Kwazulu Pineapple & Red Pepper New World Sauce (Knorr) | 52 | 0 |
| Low In Fat White Wine, Mushroom & Herb (Homepride) | 40 | 1 |
| Mushroom Alfredo (Five Brothers) | 122 | 11 |
| Mushroom & White Wine Pour Over Sauce (Knorr) | 49 | 4 |
| Napoletana Pasta Sauce (Tesco) | 49 | 1 |
| Norfolk Chicken (Colman's) | 99 | 8 |
| Oriental Sweet & Sour Sauce (Chicken Tonight) | 92 | 1 |
| Original Sauce for Bolognese (RAGU) | 51 | 0 |
| Parsley Sauce Classic Sauce Mix (Knorr) | 437 | 24 |
| Peking Stir & Sizzle Duo Jar (Chicken Tonight) | 121 | 9 |
| Pepper & Brandy Pour Over Sauce (Knorr) | 52 | 5 |
| Red Wine Cook-in-Sauce (Homepride) | 46 | 1 |
| Red Wine & Herbs (RAGU) | 62 | 2 |
| Rogan Josh Curry Cook-in-Sauce (Homepride) | 61 | 1 |
| Romano & Garlic (Five Brothers) | 74 | 3 |
| Sauce for Cottage Pie with Rich Gravy (Colman's) | 53 | 3 |
| Smoky New York American BBQ Style Sauce (Heinz) | 123 | 0 |
| Somerset Pork (Colman's) | 59 | 3 |
| Spanish Chicken Sauce (Chicken Tonight) | 49 | 1 |
| Spicy Durban Curry New World Sauce (Knorr) | 61 | 3 |
| Spicy Mediterranean Tomato Stir & Serve Sauce (Homepride) | 39 | 1 |
| Sun Dried Tomato Stir & Serve Sauce (Homepride) | 62 | 3 |
| Sweet & Sour Cook-in-Sauce (Homepride) | 92 | 0 |

| | Calories | Fat (g) |
|---|---|---|
| Sweet & Sour Stir & Sizzle Duo Jar (Chicken Tonight) | 149 | 8 |
| Tandoori Stir Fry Sauce Stir It Up (Chicken Tonight) | 633 | 58 |
| Thai Red Curry Stir & Sizzle Duo Jar (Chicken Tonight) | 183 | 18 |
| Thai Sweet Chilli Stir & Sizzle Duo Jar (Chicken Tonight) | 136 | 11 |
| Tikka Masala Curry Cook-in-Sauce (Homepride) | 112 | 6 |
| Tikka Masala Stir & Sizzle Duo Jar (Chicken Tonight) | 188 | 17 |
| Tomato Lasagne Sauce (RAGU) | 36 | 0 |
| Tomato & Basil Stir & Serve Sauce (Homepride) | 58 | 3 |
| Tomato & Basil (Five Brothers) | 60 | 3 |
| Tomato & Herb Potato Bake (Homepride) | 197 | 18 |
| Tomato & Herbs Stir Fry Sauce Stir It Up (Chicken Tonight) | 626 | 59 |
| Tomato & Onion Cook-in-Sauce (Homepride) | 48 | 1 |
| Traditional Sauce for Pasta (RAGU) | 67 | 2 |
| White Lasagne Sauce (RAGU) | 170 | 16 |
| White Sauce Classic Sauce Mix (Knorr) | 275 | 2.5 |
| White Wine & Cream Cook-in-Sauce (Homepride) | 79 | 5 |
| White Wine Gravy Bonne Cuisine Sauce (Crosse & Blackwell) | 350 | 6 |

## CRISPS & SAVOURY SNACKS

| | Calories | Fat (g) |
|---|---|---|
| Bombay Mix per 100g | 503 | 33 |
| Cashew Nuts per 100g | 619 | 51 |
| Cheese & Onion Crisps (Walkers) per 25g pack | 131 | 8 |

| | Calories | Fat (g) |
|---|---|---|
| Cheesy Wotsits per 21g pack | 114 | 7 |
| Cheesy Wotsits per 50g pack | 216 | 13 |
| Crispy Bacon Wheat Crunchies per 35g pack | 158 | 7 |
| Doritos Cool Original per 33g pack | 168 | 8.5 |
| Doritos Pizza per 33g pack | 167 | 9 |
| Doritos Tangy Cheese per 33g pack | 168 | 9 |
| French Fries Cheese & Onion (Walkers) per 19g pack | 81 | 3 |
| French Fries Ready Salted (Walkers) per 19g pack | 82 | 3 |
| Hula Hoops Original (KP) per 27g pack | 140 | 8.5 |
| Hula Hoops Salt & Vinegar (KP) per 27g pack | 137 | 8.5 |
| Lightly Salted (Walkers) per 28g pack | 132 | 6 |
| McCoys Salt & Malt Vinegar per 35g pack | 175 | 10 |
| McCoys Chedder & Onion per 35g pack | 177 | 10 |
| McCoys Flame Grilled Steak per 35g pack | 176 | 10 |
| Nice n Spicy Nik Naks per 34g pack | 185 | 11 |
| Nice n Spicy Nik Naks per 50g pack | 271 | 17 |
| Pistachio Nuts per 100g, including shells | 332 | 31 |
| Prawn Cocktail Crisps (Walkers) per 25g pack | 131 | 8 |
| Prawn Crackers per 100g | 534 | 31 |
| Ready Salted Crisps (Walkers) per 25g pack | 133 | 10 |
| Roast Chicken Crisps (Walkers) per 28g pack | 130 | 8 |
| Salt & Vinegar Crisps (Walkers) per 25g pack | 131 | 8 |
| Salt & Vinegar Wheat Crunchies per 35g pack | 158 | 7 |

| | Calories | Fat (g) |
|---|---|---|
| *Salted Peanuts per 100g* | 602 | 53 |
| *Smokey Bacon Crisps (Walkers) per 25g pack* | 131 | 8 |
| *Smokey Bacon Crisps (Walkers) per 34.5g pack* | 181 | 12 |
| *Spicy Tomato Wheat Crunchies per 35g pack* | 158 | 7 |
| *Worcester Sauce Crisps (Walkers) per 25g pack* | 131 | 8 |
| *Worcester Sauce Wheat Crunchies per 35g pack* | 158 | 7 |

## DAIRY PRODUCTS

### Cheese per 100g

| | Calories | Fat (g) |
|---|---|---|
| *Blue Stilton* | 410 | 35 |
| *Boursin – Garlic & Fine Herbs* | 406 | 41 |
| *Boursin – Light* | 183 | 12 |
| *Boursin – Poivre* | 406 | 41 |
| *Caerphilly* | 375 | 31 |
| *Camembert* | 295 | 24 |
| *Cheddar, reduced fat* | 260 | 15 |
| *Cheddar* | 410 | 35 |
| *Cheese, Low Fat, Mature (Heinz Weight Watchers)* | 182 | 5 |
| *Cheese, Low Fat, Mild (Heinz Weight Watchers)* | 182 | 5 |
| *Cheese Spread* | 275 | 23 |
| *Cream Cheese* | 440 | 17 |
| *Dairylea Light Slices, per slice* | 51 | 2.6 |
| *Dairylea Light Tub Cheese Spread* | 161 | 9 |

| | Calories | Fat (g) |
|---|---|---|
| *Dairylea Slices, per slice* | 69 | 6 |
| *Dairylea Triangle, per portion* | 32 | 3 |
| *Dairylea Tub Cheese Spread* | 217 | 17 |
| *Danish Blue* | 347 | 30 |
| *Derby* | 402 | 34 |
| *Edam* | 330 | 25 |
| *Feta* | 250 | 20 |
| *Gouda* | 375 | 31 |
| *Kraft Singles* | 260 | 19 |
| *Leicester* | 400 | 34 |
| *Parmesan* | 450 | 33 |
| *Philadelphia Full Fat Soft Cheese Tub* | 250 | 24 |
| *Philadelphia Light Medium Fat Soft Cheese* | 190 | 16 |
| *Philadelphia Light with Chives Medium Fat Soft Cheese* | 185 | 16 |
| *Philadelphia Light with Garlic & Herbs Medium Fat Soft Cheese* | 180 | 16 |
| *Philadelphia Light with Ham Medium Fat Soft Cheese* | 184 | 15 |
| *Processed Cheese* | 330 | 27 |

**Milk & Cream per 100ml**

| | | |
|---|---|---|
| *Cream, clotted* | 585 | 64 |
| *Cream, double* | 450 | 48 |
| *Cream, half* | 150 | 13 |

| | Calories | Fat(g) |
|---|---|---|
| *Cream, single* | *200* | *19* |
| *Cream, soured* | *205* | *20* |
| *Cream, whipping* | *375* | *40* |
| *Elmlea – Aerosol* | *256* | *25* |
| *Elmlea – Double* | *345* | *36* |
| *Elmlea – Light – Double* | *247* | *25* |
| *Elmlea – Light – Single* | *127* | *9* |
| *Elmlea – Light – Whipping* | *200* | *19* |
| *Elmlea – Single* | *147* | *13* |
| *Elmlea – Whipping* | *287* | *29* |
| *Evaporated Milk (Carnation)* | *151* | *9* |
| *Ideal (Nestlé)* | *160* | *9* |
| *Milk, condensed* | *330* | *10* |
| *Milk, evaporated* | *151* | *9* |
| *Milk, semi-skimmed* | *45* | *2* |
| *Milk, skimmed* | *33* | *0* |
| *Milk, whole* | *65* | *4* |
| *Simply Double (Nestlé)* | *300* | *30* |
| *Sterilised Cream (Fussells)* | *233* | *23* |
| *Tip Top (Nestlé)* | *112* | *6* |

**Butter & Spreads per 100g**

| | | |
|---|---|---|
| *Butter* | *737* | *82* |

| | Calories | Fat (g) |
|---|---|---|
| *Carapelli* | 537 | 59 |
| *Flora 70% Vegetable Fat Spread* | 630 | 70 |
| *Flora Buttery* | 630 | 70 |
| *Flora Light* | 355 | 38 |
| *Flora Low Salt* | 630 | 70 |
| *Gold Low Fat* | 359 | 38 |
| *Gold Lowest* | 259 | 27 |
| *Gold Unsalted* | 360 | 38 |
| *Golden Churn* | 628 | 69 |
| *I Can't Believe It's Not Butter* | 630 | 70 |
| *Margarine* | 739 | 82 |
| *Olivio with Olive Oil* | 536 | 59 |
| *Olivite, Low Fat Spread with Olive Oil* (Heinz Weight Watchers) | 351 | 39 |
| *Stork, packet* | 720 | 80 |
| *Stork, tub* | 660 | 73 |
| *Summer Country* | 496 | 55 |
| *Utterly Butterly* | 615 | 67 |
| *Vitalite* | 578 | 63 |

## DRESSINGS per 100ml

| | | |
|---|---|---|
| *95% Fat Free* (Hellmann's) | 111 | 5 |
| *95% Herb & Garlic* (Hellmann's) | 116 | 5 |
| *Caesar Dressing* (Hellmann's) | 499 | 52 |

| | Calories | Fat(g) |
|---|---|---|
| *Creamy Italian Dressing (Hellmann's)* | 460 | 47 |
| *Fat Free French Vinaigrette Dressing (Kraft)* | 39 | 0 |
| *Fat Free Thousand Island Dressing (Kraft)* | 90 | 0 |
| *Garlic & Herb Dressing Reduced Calorie (Hellmann's)* | 232 | 19 |
| *Italian & Garlic Vinaigrette Dressing (Kraft)* | 128 | 11 |
| *Low Fat Dressing, Blue Cheese Flavoured (Heinz Weight Watchers)* | 59 | 3 |
| *Low Fat Dressing, Caesar Style (Heinz Weight Watchers)* | 60 | 3 |
| *Low Fat Dressing, Mild Mustard (Heinz Weight Watchers)* | 63 | 4 |
| *Low Fat French Dressing (Hellmann's)* | 62 | 2 |
| *Luxury French Dressing (Hellmann's)* | 296 | 26 |
| *Mayonnaise-Style Dressing 90% Fat Free (Heinz Weight Watchers)* | 125 | 9 |
| *Original Thousand Island Dressing (Kraft)* | 365 | 32 |
| *Ranch Dressing with Blue Cheese (Kraft)* | 485 | 50 |
| *Ranch Dressing (Kraft)* | 420 | 42 |
| *Salad Cream Style Dressing (Heinz Weight Watchers)* | 115 | 4 |
| *Thousand Island Dressing Reduced Calorie (Hellmann's)* | 259 | 19 |
| *Thousand Island Dressing (Hellmann's)* | 347 | 31 |

## DRINKS per 100ml

| | | |
|---|---|---|
| *Apple & Strawberry Squash (Robinsons)* | 10 | 0 |
| *Blackcurrant Cordial, diluted* | 52 | 0 |

| | Calories | Fat (g) |
|---|---|---|
| *Caffeine Free Diet Coke* | 0.4 | 0 |
| *Coca-Cola* | 43 | 0 |
| *Cola (Virgin)* | 44 | 0 |
| *Diet Coke* | 0.4 | 0 |
| *Diet Cola (Virgin)* | 0.4 | 0 |
| *Diet Dr Pepper* | 0.6 | 0 |
| *Diet Fanta (Schweppes)* | 3 | 0 |
| *Diet Lemonade (Schweppes)* | 2 | 0 |
| *Diet Lemonade (R Whites)* | 1.4 | 0 |
| *Dr Pepper* | 41 | 0 |
| *Ginger Beer (Tesco)* | 58 | 0 |
| *Fruit & Barley Pear Juice Drink (Robinsons)* | 19 | 0 |
| *Grape, Blackcurrant, Raspberry Juice Drink (Ribena)* | 30 | 0 |
| *Ginger Beer (Old Jamaica)* | 64 | 0 |
| *Lemonade, homemade* | 141 | 0 |
| *Lemonade, sparkling* | 42 | 0 |
| *Lemonade (Tesco)* | 15 | 0 |
| *Lime Juice Cordial (Princes)* | 25 | 0 |
| *Lucozade* | 73 | 0 |
| *No Added Sugar Cherry Squash (Robinsons)* | 10 | 0 |
| *No Added Sugar Lemon Squash (Robinsons)* | 10 | 0 |
| *No Added Sugar Orange Squash (Robinsons)* | 16 | 0 |
| *No Added Sugar Apple & Blackcurrant Squash (Princes)* | 13 | 0 |

| | Calories | Fat (g) |
|---|---|---|
| Orange Cordial *(Princes)* | 58 | 0 |
| Orange Squash, low calorie | 48 | 0 |
| Orange & Pineapple Squash *(Robinsons)* | 56 | 0 |
| Orange High Juice *(Robinsons)* | 182 | 0 |
| Pear & Blackcurrant Squash *(Kia-Ora)* | 57 | 0 |
| Peach High Juice *(Robinsons)* | 181 | 0 |
| Perfectly Clear Strawberry *(Silver Springs)* | 0.8 | 0 |
| Perfectly Clear Strawberry *(Silver Springs)* | 0.8 | 0 |
| Pink Grapefruit High Juice *(Robinsons)* | 190 | 0 |
| Slimline Tonic Water *(Schweppes)* | 2 | 0 |
| Soda Water *(Schweppes)* | 0 | 0 |
| Tango Apple | 4.5 | 0 |
| Diet Tango Tropical | 4.0 | 0 |
| Vimto Grape | 30 | 0 |
| Vimto Blackcurrant | 30 | 0 |
| Vimto Raspberry | 30 | 0 |

### Hot Drinks per cup, 200ml (1 tsp sugar – 19cal, 0g fat)

| | Calories | Fat (g) |
|---|---|---|
| Cappuccino, with whole milk | 89 | 5 |
| Cappuccino, with skimmed milk | 50 | 0 |
| Coffee, decafinated, black | 0 | 0 |
| Coffee, filtered, black | 7 | 0 |
| Coffee, ground with whole milk (25ml) | 23 | 1 |

| | Calories | Fat (g) |
|---|---|---|
| *Coffee, ground with skimmed milk (25ml)* | 18 | 0 |
| *Coffee, instant with whole milk (25ml)* | 18 | 1 |
| *Coffee, instant with skimmed milk (25ml)* | 13 | 0 |
| *Coffee-Mate, per serving (Carnation)* | 35 | 2 |
| *Hot Chocolate (Semi Skimmed Milk)* | 71 | 2 |
| *Tea, black* | 1 | 0 |
| *Tea, with whole milk (25ml)* | 18 | 4 |
| *Tea, with skimmed milk (25ml)* | 13 | 2 |

## Fruit Juice per 100ml

| | Calories | Fat (g) |
|---|---|---|
| *Five Alive Blackcurrant* | 62 | 0 |
| *Five Alive Citrus* | 50 | 0 |
| *Five Alive Orange Breakfast* | 46 | 0 |
| *Five Alive Tropical* | 41 | 0 |
| *Five Alive Very Berry* | 53 | 0 |
| *Ocean Spray* | 183 | 0 |
| *Grapefruit Juice* | 40 | 0 |
| *Hi Juice 66 (Schweppes)* | 52 | 0 |
| *Libby's Orange C* | 48 | 0 |
| *Orange Juice* | 45 | 0 |
| *Orange Juice Peach & Apricot (Del Monte)* | 44 | 0 |
| *Orange Juice Standard (Schweppes)* | 46 | 0 |
| *Pineapple Juice (Del Monte)* | 41 | 0 |

| | Calories | Fat(g) |
|---|---|---|
| *Pineapple Juice (Schweppes)* | 56 | 0 |
| *Pink Grapefruit Juice* | 34 | 0 |
| *Pink Grapefruit Juice (Schweppes)* | 43 | 0 |
| *Pure Apple Juice (Del Monte)* | 48 | 0 |
| *Purple Grape & Blackcurrant Juice (Welch's)* | 48 | 0 |
| *Ribena Blackcurrant* | 44 | 0 |
| *Ribena Light Blackcurrant* | 1 | 0 |
| *Sweetened Grapefruit Juice (Schweppes)* | 57 | 0 |
| *Tomato Juice Cocktail (Schweppes)* | 24 | 0 |
| *Tropicana Pure Orange Juice* | 43 | 0 |

**Milkshakes per 100ml**

| | Calories | Fat(g) |
|---|---|---|
| *Banana Nesquik (Nestlé) made with whole milk* | 428 | 5 |
| *Banana Nesquik (Nestlé) made with semi-skimmed milk* | 395 | 1 |
| *Chocolate Nesquik (Nestlé) made with whole milk* | 171 | 8 |
| *Chocolate Nesquik (Nestlé) made with semi-skimmed milk* | 155 | 4 |
| *Strawberry Nesquik (Nestlé) made with whole milk* | 168 | 8 |
| *Strawberry Nesquik (Nestlé) made with semi-skimmed milk* | 155 | 3 |

**EGGS** – per 50g egg

| | Calories | Fat(g) |
|---|---|---|
| *Eggs, medium* | 85 | 6.3 |
| *Eggs, boiled or poached* | 73.5 | 6 |
| *Eggs, fried* | 90 | 7 |

| | Calories | Fat (g) |
|---|---|---|
| Eggs, raw, white only | 17.5 | 0 |
| Eggs, raw, whole | 73.5 | 6 |
| Eggs, raw, yolk only | 170 | 15 |
| Eggs, scrambled, per 100g | 247 | 22 |

### FISH per 100g

| | Calories | Fat (g) |
|---|---|---|
| Cod fillet, grilled, baked or poached | 95 | 1 |
| Cod fillet, in batter, fried in oil | 200 | 10 |
| Coley fillet, grilled, baked or poached | 105 | 1 |
| Crab, boiled | 127 | 5 |
| Fish Cakes, fried | 188 | 11 |
| Haddock, fried in breadcrumbs | 175 | 8 |
| Haddock, steamed | 100 | 1 |
| Halibut fillet, poached | 130 | 4 |
| Herrings, fried | 235 | 15 |
| Herrings, grilled | 200 | 13 |
| Kippers | 205 | 11 |
| Lemon Sole, fried in breadcrumbs | 215 | 13 |
| Lemon Sole, steamed | 91 | 1 |
| Mussels, boiled or steamed | 87 | 2 |
| Plaice, fried in crumbs | 230 | 13 |
| Plaice, steamed | 93 | 2 |
| Salmon, smoked | 147 | 5 |

| | Calories | Fat (g) |
|---|---|---|
| *Salmon, steamed* | 197 | 13 |
| *Whitebait, fried* | 525 | 47 |
| *Whiting, in breadcrumbs, fried in oil* | 190 | 10 |
| *Whiting, steamed* | 90 | 1 |

## FROZEN FOODS per item

| | Calories | Fat (g) |
|---|---|---|
| *100% Best Beef Burger (Birds Eye)* | 188 | 17 |
| *Beef Grillsteaks (Birds Eye)* | 264 | 22 |
| *Beef Quarter Pounders (Birds Eye)* | 317 | 26 |
| *Chicken Burger (Birds Eye)* | 158 | 9 |
| *Chicken O's (Birds Eye)* | 78 | 5 |
| *Chicken Quarter Pounders (Birds Eye)* | 282 | 16 |
| *Chicksticks (Birds Eye)* | 191 | 11 |
| *Crispy Chicken Dippers (Birds Eye)* | 50 | 4 |
| *Crispy Chicken (Birds Eye)* | 219 | 13 |
| *Crispy Vegetable Fingers (Birds Eye)* | 48 | 2 |
| *Crunchy Garlic Chicken (Birds Eye)* | 262 | 15 |
| *Garlic Chargrills (Birds Eye)* | 211 | 15 |
| *Lamb Grillsteaks (Birds Eye)* | 203 | 15 |
| *Lamb Quarter Pounders (Birds Eye)* | 249 | 17 |
| *Mega Burgers (Birds Eye)* | 442 | 35 |
| *Mighty Beef Grillsteaks (Birds Eye)* | 449 | 36 |
| *Original Chargrills (Birds Eye)* | 216 | 16 |

| | Calories | Fat (g) |
|---|---|---|
| *Original Vegetable Rice* (Birds Eye) per 100g | 105 | 1 |
| *Original & Best Beef Burger* (Birds Eye) | 158 | 13 |
| *Pork Quarter Pounders* (Birds Eye) | 272 | 22 |
| *Vegetable Quarter Pounders* (Birds Eye) | 189 | 9 |

## Vegetables per 100g

| | | |
|---|---|---|
| *Broad Beans, boiled* | 81 | 1 |
| *Broccoli Spears* | 31 | 1 |
| *Brussels Sprouts, boiled* | 35 | 1 |
| *Cabbage, shredded* | 26 | 0 |
| *Carrots, boiled* | 24 | 0 |
| *Cauliflower, boiled* | 29 | 1 |
| *Cauliflower, Peas & Carrots* (Birds Eye) | 32 | 0 |
| *Garden Peas* (Birds Eye) | 62 | 1 |
| *Green Beans, boiled* | 25 | 0 |
| *Original Mixed Vegetables* (Birds Eye) | 46 | 1 |
| *Peas, boiled* | 69 | 1 |
| *Petits Pois* (Birds Eye) | 62 | 1 |
| *Sweetcorn, kernels* | 109 | 2 |

## Chips & Potatoes per 100g

| | | |
|---|---|---|
| *Alphabites* (Birds Eye) | 134 | 5 |
| *Crispy Potato Fritters* (Birds Eye) | 145 | 8 |

| | Calories | Fat (g) |
|---|---|---|
| *Fish & Chips (Ross)* | 168 | 9 |
| *Gold Standard Crinkle Cut Fries,* | | |
| *deep fried in vegetable oil (McCain)* | 192 | 8 |
| *Gold Standard Crinkle Cut Fries,* | | |
| *frozen raw product (McCain)* | 127 | 4 |
| *Gold Standard Straight Cut Fries,* | | |
| *deep fried in vegetable oil (McCain)* | 225 | 9 |
| *Hash Browns, deep fried in vegetable oil (McCain) 54g* | 133 | 8 |
| *Hash Browns, frozen raw product (McCain) 54g* | 94 | 4 |
| *Hash Browns, oven baked product (McCain) 54g* | 106 | 5 |
| *House of Horror, frozen raw product (McCain)* | 188 | 7 |
| *House of Horror, oven baked product (McCain)* | 222 | 9 |
| *New Crinkle Cut Oven Chips, oven baked product (McCain)* | 187 | 6 |
| *New Straight Cut Oven Chips, frozen raw product (McCain)* | 154 | 4 |
| *New Straight Cut Oven Chips, oven baked product (McCain)* | 172 | 5 |
| *Potato Smiles, deep fried in vegetable oil (McCain)* | 227 | 10 |
| *Potato Smiles, frozen raw product (McCain)* | 192 | 7 |
| *Potato Smiles, oven baked product (McCain)* | 220 | 9 |
| *Potato Speedsters, deep fried in vegetable oil (McCain)* | 216 | 9 |
| *Potato Speedsters, oven baked product (McCain)* | 233 | 9 |
| *Potato Waffles (Birds Eye) per piece* | 95 | 5 |
| *Southern Fries Straight Cut,* | | |
| *deep fried in vegetable oil (McCain)* | 246 | 13 |

| | Calories | Fat(g) |
|---|---|---|
| *Southern Fries Straight Cut, frozen raw product (McCain)* | 182 | 8 |
| *Southern Fries Straight Cut, oven baked product (McCain)* | 263 | 11 |
| *Spicy Wedges, deep fried in vegetable oil (McCain)* | 187 | 8 |
| *Spicy Wedges, oven baked product (McCain)* | 219 | 8 |

### Fish per item

| | Calories | Fat(g) |
|---|---|---|
| *100% Cod Fillet Fish Fingers (Birds Eye)* | 170 | 7 |
| *100% Fish Fillet Fish Fingers (Birds Eye)* | 200 | 12 |
| *Battered Fish Portions (Ross)* | 223 | 12 |
| *Big Time Cod Cakes (Birds Eye)* | 185 | 8 |
| *Captain's Cod Pie (Birds Eye) per serving* | 432 | 24 |
| *Captain's Coins (Birds Eye)* | 38 | 2 |
| *Cod Fillet Fish Fingers (Birds Eye)* | 56 | 2 |
| *Cod Portions (Tesco)* | 189 | 8 |
| *Cod Steaks in Butter Sauce (Birds Eye)* | 165 | 8 |
| *Cod Steaks in Cheese Sauce (Birds Eye)* | 96 | 4 |
| *Cod Steaks in Crispy Batter (Birds Eye)* | 192 | 12 |
| *Cod Steaks in Crunch Crumbs (Birds Eye)* | 215 | 13 |
| *Cod Steaks in Parsley Sauce (Birds Eye)* | 160 | 5 |
| *Extra Large Haddock Fillets approved by Harry Ramsdens (Young's Chip Shop)* | 235 | 14 |
| *Extra Large Plaice Fillets approved by Harry Ramsdens (Young's Chip Shop)* | 252 | 18 |

| | Calories | Fat (g) |
|---|---|---|
| *Fish Cakes, cod (Tesco)* | 79 | 3 |
| *Fish Fingers in Crispy Batter (Birds Eye)* | 68 | 4 |
| *Fish Fingers, Cod Fillet (Birds Eye)* | 56 | 2 |
| *Fish in Pastry – Cheese (Birds Eye)* | 351 | 20 |
| *Haddock Fillet Fish Fingers (Birds Eye)* | 56 | 2 |
| *Haddock Steaks in Crispy Batter (Birds Eye)* | 192 | 12 |
| *Haddock Steaks in Crunch Crumbs (Birds Eye)* | 215 | 13 |
| *Regular Cod Fillets approved by* | | |
| *Harry Ramsdens (Young's Chip Shop)* | 237 | 14 |
| *Salmon Fish Cakes (Birds Eye)* | 84 | 5 |
| *Salmon & Broccoli Pie (Birds Eye)* | 435 | 20 |
| *Simply Fish in Crispy Batter (Birds Eye)* | 215 | 9 |
| *Simply Fish in Seasoned Breadcrumbs (Birds Eye)* | 192 | 8 |

## Ice Cream

| | Calories | Fat (g) |
|---|---|---|
| *Bugs Pops Lolly (50g lolly), each* | 48 | 0 |
| *Calippo Mini Lemon/Lime, each* | 60 | 0 |
| *Calippo Mini Orange, each* | 60 | 0 |
| *Calippo Orange, each* | 100 | 0 |
| *Calippo Mini, 60g* | 20 | 0 |
| *Carte d'Or Caramel, per 100ml* | 120 | 5 |
| *Carte d'Or Chocolate, per 100ml* | 125 | 6 |
| *Carte d'Or Coconut, per 100ml* | 130 | 8 |

| | Calories | Fat(g) |
|---|---|---|
| *Carte d'Or Stracciatella, per 100ml* | 130 | 5 |
| *Carte d'Or Strawberry, per 100ml* | 105 | 4 |
| *Carte d'Or Vanilla, per 100ml* | 110 | 5 |
| *Chunky Choc bar (Wall's), each* | 163 | 11 |
| *Cornetto Classico (choc & nut), each* | 225 | 12 |
| *Cornetto Mint choc chip, each* | 225 | 12 |
| *Cornetto Strawberry, each* | 190 | 8 |
| *Cream of Cornish (Wall's), per 100ml* | 90 | 4 |
| *Feast, each* | 315 | 23 |
| *Feast Mini (Chocolate), each* | 195 | 14 |
| *Feast Mini (Toffee), each* | 190 | 14 |
| *Fruit Pastil Lolly (65ml lolly), each* | 57 | 0 |
| *Fruit Pastil Lolly (75ml lolly), each* | 66 | 0 |
| *Kit Kat Chunky (65g bar), each* | 260 | 15 |
| *Magnum Classic, each* | 280 | 17 |
| *Magnum Classic Mini, each* | 170 | 11 |
| *Magnum Cone, each* | 350 | 22 |
| *Magnum Double Caramel, each* | 340 | 21 |
| *Magnum Double Chocolate, each* | 371 | 25 |
| *Magnum White, each* | 300 | 20 |
| *Magnum White Mini, each* | 175 | 11 |
| *Mini Milk – Chocolate, Strawberry or Vanilla, each* | 35 | 1 |
| *Popsicle, 25ml* | 6 | 0 |

| | Calories | Fat (g) |
|---|---|---|
| *Smarties Pop-up Lolly (55g lolly), each* | 140 | 5 |
| *Soft Scoop Vanilla Light (Wall's), per 100ml* | 80 | 3 |
| *Soft Scoop Vanilla (Wall's), per 100ml* | 85 | 4 |
| *Solero Exotic, each* | 115 | 3 |
| *Solero Ice, each* | 65 | 2 |
| *Strawberry Split, each* | 125 | 4 |
| *Too Good To Be True Chocolate (Wall's), per 100ml* | 75 | 1 |
| *Too Good To Be True Toffee (Wall's), per 100ml* | 75 | 1 |
| *Too Good To Be True Vanilla (Wall's), per 100ml* | 70 | 0 |
| *Twister, each* | 90 | 2 |
| *Twister Mini, each* | 50 | 1 |
| *Viennetta Biscuit Caramel, per 100ml* | 180 | 12 |
| *Viennetta Lemon, per 100ml* | 130 | 8 |
| *Viennetta Mint, per 100ml* | 135 | 9 |
| *Viennetta Original Vanilla, per 100ml* | 130 | 9 |
| *Viennetta Strawberry Cheesecake, per 100ml* | 180 | 12 |
| *Wall's Fives Chocolate, per 100ml* | 90 | 4 |
| *Wall's Fives Fruit Flavours, per 100ml* | 90 | 4 |
| *Walls Neopolitan, per 100ml* | 81 | 4 |
| *Walls Ribbon Vanilla, per 100ml* | 90 | 5 |
| *Walls Ribbon Vanilla Light, per 100ml* | 80 | 3 |
| *Walls Ribbon Vanilla sliceable, per 100ml* | 90 | 4 |

Calories Fat (g)

## FRUIT

**Fat figures are given to the nearest half gram up to three grams and to the nearest gram thereafter**

| | Calories | Fat (g) |
|---|---|---|
| Apples, cooking stewed with sugar (per 100g) | 74 | 0 |
| Apples, cooking, raw, 1 average (200g) | 70 | 0 |
| Apples, eating, raw, 1 average (150g) | 68 | 0 |
| Apricots, raw, 1 (45g) | 14 | 0 |
| Bananas, raw, 1 (150g) | 143 | 1 |
| Blackcurrants, raw (per 100g) | 28 | 0 |
| Damsons, raw with stones (per 100g) | 35 | 0 |
| Dates, with stones (per 100g) | 225 | 0 |
| Figs (per 100g) | 227 | 2 |
| Gooseberries, raw (per 100g) | 19 | 0 |
| Gooseberries, stewed with sugar (per 100g) | 54 | 0 |
| Grapefruit, 1/2 (110g) | 30 | 0 |
| Grapes, seedless (per 100g) | 60 | 0 |
| Kiwi Fruit, 1 (75g) | 37 | 0 |
| Lemons, 1 (70g) | 13 | 0 |
| Lychees, raw (per 100g) | 58 | 0 |
| Mangoes, 1/2 (75g) | 43 | 0 |
| Melon, Cantaloupe, 100g slice | 20 | 0 |
| Melon, Honeydew, 100g slice | 28 | 0 |
| Melon, Watermelon, 100g slice | 11 | 0 |

| | Calories | Fat (g) |
|---|---|---|
| *Nectarines 1 peeled (75g)* | 30 | 0 |
| *Oranges, 1 peeled (200g)* | 70 | 0 |
| *Peaches, 1 average (150g)* | 50 | 0 |
| *Pears, 1 (150g)* | 60 | 0 |
| *Pineapple, 100g slice* | 40 | 0 |
| *Plums, 1 (75g)* | 26 | 0 |
| *Raspberries, raw (per 100g)* | 25 | 0 |
| *Raspberries, cooked with sugar (per 100g)* | 48 | 0 |
| *Rhubarb, stewed with sugar (per 100g)* | 47 | 0 |
| *Satsumas, 1 peeled (130g)* | 46 | 0 |
| *Strawberries (per 100g)* | 27 | 0 |
| *Tangerines, 1 peeled (130g)* | 46 | 0 |

## JAMS & PRESERVES – per tablespoon = 25g

| | Calories | Fat (g) |
|---|---|---|
| *American Stripey Choc Peanut Butter (Sunpat)* | 155 | 12 |
| *Apricot Jam* | 61 | 0 |
| *Apricot Spread (Heinz Weight Watchers)* | 27 | 0 |
| *Blackcurrant Spread (Heinz Weight Watchers)* | 26 | 0 |
| *Chocolate Spread* | 142 | 9 |
| *Clear Honey (Gales)* | 73 | 0 |
| *Creamy Big Crunch Peanut Butter (Sunpat)* | 151 | 12 |
| *Creamy Smooth Peanut Butter (Sunpat)* | 155 | 13 |
| *Jam* | 65 | 0 |

| | Calories | Fat(g) |
|---|---|---|
| *Lemon Curd* | 71 | 1 |
| *Marmalade* | 65 | 0 |
| *Original Crunchy Peanut Butter (Sunpat)* | 157 | 13 |
| *Original Smooth Peanut Butter (Sunpat)* | 156 | 13 |
| *Plum Jam* | 65 | 0 |
| *Raspberry Jam* | 65 | 0 |
| *Raspberry Spread (Heinz Weight Watchers)* | 27 | 0 |
| *Set Honey (Gales)* | 72 | 0 |
| *Seville Orange Spread (Heinz Weight Watchers)* | 27 | 0 |
| *Stawberry Jam* | 65 | 0 |
| *Strawberry Spread (Heinz Weight Watchers)* | 28 | 0 |
| *Marmite* | 43 | 0 |

## MEAT per 100g unless stated

### Fat figures are given to the nearest half gram up to three grams and to the nearest gram thereafter

| | Calories | Fat(g) |
|---|---|---|
| *Bacon, back, fried, 1 slice, 10g* | 47 | 4 |
| *Bacon, back, grilled, 1 slice, 10g* | 31 | 3 |
| *Bacon, middle, fried, 1 slice, 10g* | 37 | 3 |
| *Bacon, middle, grilled, 1 slice, 10g* | 32 | 2 |
| *Bacon, streaky, fried, 1 slice, 10g* | 50 | 5 |
| *Bacon, streaky, grilled, 1 slice, 10g* | 43 | 4 |
| *Beef, mince, stewed* | 230 | 15 |

| | Calories | Fat (g) |
|---|---|---|
| *Beef, rib, roast* | 350 | 28 |
| *Beef, rump steak, fried, 175g* | 438 | 26 |
| *Beef, rump steak, lean, grilled, 175g* | 334 | 12 |
| *Beef, sirloin, roast* | 284 | 21 |
| *Beef, stewing steak, stewed* | 225 | 10 |
| *Chicken, breaded, fried in oil* | 240 | 13 |
| *Chicken, drumsticks, no skin, baked, 2* | 179 | 9 |
| *Chicken, meat & skin, roasted* | 216 | 14 |
| *Chicken, meat only, roasted* | 150 | 5 |
| *Chicken nuggets, 1, 20g* | 57 | 4 |
| *Duck, roast, meat only* | 190 | 10 |
| *Duck, roast, meat, fat & skin* | 340 | 30 |
| *Gammon, joint, boiled* | 269 | 19 |
| *Goose, roast* | 320 | 22 |
| *Ham leg, fresh, lean, 2 slices, 46g* | 50 | 1.5 |
| *Ham shoulder, 2 slices, 50g* | 55 | 3 |
| *Kidney, lamb, fried* | 155 | 6 |
| *Lamb cutlets, lean, grilled, 1, 30g* | 70 | 4 |
| *Lamb chump, chops, lean, grilled, 1, 55g* | 111 | 5 |
| *Lamb, leg, lean, baked, 2 slices, 80g* | 158 | 5 |
| *Lamb, shoulder lean, baked, 1 slice, 25g* | 46 | 2 |
| *Liver, calf, fried* | 255 | 13 |
| *Liver, chicken, fried* | 195 | 11 |

| | Calories | Fat (g) |
|---|---|---|
| *Liver, lamb, fried,* | 230 | 14 |
| *Pork chops, grilled* | 332 | 25 |
| *Pork leg, roast* | 285 | 20 |
| *Salami, 50g* | 214 | 19 |
| *Sausage Rolls, 1, 130g* | 371 | 23 |
| *Sausages, Beef, grilled, 1, 50g* | 127 | 9 |
| *Sausages, Pork, thin, grilled, 2, 100g* | 283 | 22 |
| *Saveloy* | 260 | 20 |
| *Turkey, roast, meat & skin* | 170 | 6 |
| *Turkey, roast, meat only* | 140 | 2.5 |

## NOODLES

| | Calories | Fat (g) |
|---|---|---|
| *Bacon Flavour SuperNoodles (Batchelors) per pack* | 480 | 21 |
| *Barbecue Beef Flavour SuperNoodles (Batchelors) per pack* | 474 | 21 |
| *Barbecue Pot Noodle per pot* | 485 | 14 |
| *BBQ Beef Micro Noodle (Knorr) per pot* | 501 | 24 |
| *Beef & Tomato Pot Noodle per pot* | 382 | 14 |
| *Black Bean & Roasted Pepper Stir In Noodle Sauce (Sharwood, per 100g)* | 122 | 4 |
| *Burger Fun Pot Noodle per pot* | 248 | 9 |
| *Chicken Micro Noodle (Knorr) per pot* | 498 | 24 |
| *Chicken & Mushroom Fun Pot Noodle per pot* | 254 | 9 |
| *Chicken & Mushroom Pot Noodle per pot* | 389 | 14 |

| | Calories | Fat (g) |
|---|---|---|
| Chinese Chow Mein Flavour SuperNoodles (Batchelors) per packet | 481 | 21 |
| Chow Mein Micro Noodle (Knorr) per pot | 492 | 23 |
| Chow Mein Pot Noodle per pot | 385 | 14 |
| Hot Chicken Curry Pot Noodle per pot | 383 | 14 |
| Italian Tomato & Herbs Flavour SuperNoodles (Batchelors) per 100g pack | 479 | 21 |
| Lemongrass & Coconut Stir In Noodle Sauce (Sharwood, per 100g) | 202 | 18 |
| Malaysian Curry Stir In Noodle Sauce (Sharwood per, 100g) | 120 | 6 |
| Medium Noodles (Sharwood, per 100g) | 340 | 2 |
| Mild Curry Flavour SuperNoodles (Batchelors) per pack | 480 | 21 |
| Mild Curry Micro Noodle (Knorr) per pot | 494 | 24 |
| Mushroom Flavour SuperNoodles (Batchelors) per pack | 477 | 21 |
| Nice'n'Spicy Fun Pot Noodle per pot | 255 | 10 |
| Nice'n'Spicy Pot Noodle per pot | 380 | 15 |
| Pizza Flavour Pot Noodle per pot | 388 | 15 |
| Sausage & Tomato Pot Noodle per pot | 389 | 14 |
| Spicy Curry Pot Noodle per pot | 379 | 14 |
| Sweet Chilli & Garlic Stir In Noodle Sauce (Sharwood, per 100g) | 107 | 3 |
| Sweet & Sour Flavour SuperNoodles (Batchelors) per pack | 478 | 21 |
| Sweet & Sour Pot Noodle per pot | 376 | 14 |

| | Calories | Fat (g) |
|---|---|---|
| *Thai Rice Noodles (Sharwood, per 100g)* | 361 | 1 |
| *Thick Noodles (Sharwood, per 100g)* | 340 | 2 |
| *Thread Noodles (Sharwood, per 100g)* | 340 | 2 |

## NUTS & RAISINS per 100g

**Fat figures are given to the nearest half gram up to three grams and to the nearest gram thereafter**

| | Calories | Fat (g) |
|---|---|---|
| *Cashew Nuts, roasted* | 610 | 51 |
| *Currants, dried* | 267 | 0.5 |
| *Peanuts, salted* | 602 | 53 |
| *Pecan Nuts* | 690 | 70 |
| *Pistachio Nuts, with shells* | 330 | 30 |
| *Raisins* | 272 | 0.5 |
| *Seedless Raisins* | 330 | 1 |
| *Sultanas* | 275 | 0.5 |
| *Walnuts* | 687 | 68 |

## OILS & FATS per 100g

| | Calories | Fat (g) |
|---|---|---|
| *Beef Dripping* | 890 | 99 |
| *Cookeen Cooking Fat* | 900 | 100 |
| *Corn Oil, per tbsp* | 133 | 15 |
| *Lard* | 890 | 99 |
| *Olive Oil, per tbsp* | 123 | 14 |

| | Calories | Fat(g) |
|---|---|---|
| *Sunflower Oil, per tbsp* | 133 | 15 |
| *Vegetable Ghee* | 897 | 99 |
| *White Flora* | 900 | 100 |

## PASTA

| | Calories | Fat(g) |
|---|---|---|
| *Cheese & Garlic Pasta 'n' Sauce (Batchelors) per pack* | 429 | 6 |
| *Cheese, Leek & Ham Pasta 'n' Sauce (Batchelors) per pack* | 478 | 7 |
| *Cheesy Pasta (Kraft) made up (per 100g)* | 230 | 11 |
| *Creamy Chicken & Sweetcorn Pasta Snack Stops (Crosse & Blackwell) per pack* | 100 | 4 |
| *Chicken & Mushroom Pasta 'n' Sauce (Batchelors) per pack* | 455 | 3 |
| *Creamy Tomato & Mushroom Pasta 'n' Sauce (Batchelors) per pack* | 458 | 4 |
| *Dried Pasta, all shapes (Napolina, per 100g)* | 352 | 2 |
| *Dried Pasta, cooked weight, all shapes (per 100g)* | 104 | 1 |
| *Dried Spaghetti, raw weight, (per 100g)* | 342 | 2 |
| *Dried Pasta, raw weight, all shapes (Buitoni, per 100g)* | 362 | 2 |
| *Fresh Egg Pasta cooked all shapes (per 100g)* | 118 | 1 |
| *Fresh Pasta Cappalletti with Chicken & Smoked Ham, cooked (per 100g)* | 162 | 4 |
| *Fresh Pasta Tortelloni with Five Cheeses, cooked (per 100g)* | 183 | 6 |
| *Italian Herb & Garlic Flavour Pasta 'n' Sauce (Batchelors) per pack* | 379 | 3 |
| *Lasagne Verdi (spinach), cooked weight (Buitoni, per 100g)* | 149 | 0 |

| | Calories | Fat(g) |
|---|---|---|
| *Lasagne Verdi (spinach), raw weight (per 100g)* | *346* | *2* |
| *Macaroni Cheese Flavour Pasta 'n' Sauce (Batchelors) per pack* | *435* | *7* |
| *Mild Cheese & Broccoli Pasta 'n' Sauce (Batchelors) per pack* | *479* | *6* |
| *Pot Pasta Nice 'n' Cheesy (per 100g)* | *379* | *8* |
| *Pot Pasta Spicy Tomato (per 100g)* | *331* | *2* |
| *Tomato & Bacon Flavour Pasta 'n' Sauce (Batchelors) per pack* | *476* | *4* |
| *Tomato & Herb Pasta Snack Stops (Crosse & Blackwell) per pack* | *201* | *3* |
| *Tomato, Onion & Herb Flavour Pasta 'n' Sauce (Batchelors) per pack* | *470* | *6* |

### PIZZAS per serving

| | Calories | Fat(g) |
|---|---|---|
| *Bagel Bites, Cheese & Pepperoni (Heinz) 3 bagels* | *154* | *7* |
| *Bagel Bites, Cheese & Tomato (Heinz) 3 bagels* | *140* | *5* |
| *Baked Beans Pizza with Cheese (Heinz) half pizza* | *459* | *12* |
| *Baked Beans Pizza with Sausage (Heinz) half pizza* | *425* | *11* |
| *Chilled Thin & Crispy Cheese & Tomato Pizza (Asda)* | *828* | *36* |
| *Chilled Thin & Crispy Ham & Pineapple Pizza (Asda)* | *834* | *26* |
| *Chilled Thin & Crispy Cheese & Tomato Pizza (Express) quarter pizza* | *142* | *3* |
| *Chilled Thin & Crispy Ham & Mushroom Pizza (Asda)* | *754* | *26* |
| *Chilled Thin & Crispy Meat Feast Pizza (Asda)* | *835* | *31* |
| *Ciabatta Ham & Mushroom Pizza (Goodfella) half pizza* | *437* | *20* |
| *Freschetta Pepperoni Pizza* | *825* | *33* |
| *Frozen Deep Pan Dish Triple Cheese Pizza (Chicago Town)* | *473* | *21* |

| | Calories | Fat(g) |
|---|---|---|
| *Frozen Deep Pan Ham & Mushroom Pizza (Chicago Town)* | 400 | 15 |
| *Frozen Ham & Pineapple Pizza (Chicago Town)* | 406 | 15 |
| *Frozen Pepperoni Pizza (Chicago Town)* | 496 | 25 |
| *Frozen Thin & Crispy Vegetable Pizza (Asda)* | 727 | 6 |
| *Pizza Fingers (McCain) 10 pack* | 750 | 23 |
| *Thin & Crispy Cheese Pizza (Goodfella) quarter pizza* | 151 | 7 |
| *Thin & Crispy Baked Beans with Pepperoni Pizza (Goodfella) quarter pizza* | 229 | 13 |

### Pizza Bases & Toppings per Base/ 300g topping

| | | |
|---|---|---|
| *Authentic Italian Bases (Napolina)* | 437 | 5 |
| *Mini - Bases (Napolina)* | 218 | 2 |
| *Mini Thin & Crispy Bases (Napolina)* | 218 | 3 |
| *Tomato with Herbs Topping (Napolina)* | 234 | 12 |
| *Tomato with Pepper & Spice Topping (Napolina)* | 186 | 9 |
| *Traditional Tomato (Napolina)* | 183 | 9 |

### PUDDINGS per serving

| | | |
|---|---|---|
| *Apple Crumble with Sultanas (Heinz Weight Watchers)* | 177 | 4 |
| *Apple Turnovers (Daelmans)* | 138 | 6 |
| *Apple & Blackcurrant Pies (Mr Kipling)* | 221 | 9 |
| *Apple & Cinnamon Danish Twist (Entermans)* | 165 | 2.4 |
| *Banoffee Pie (Tesco)* | 383 | 18 |

| | Calories | Fat(g) |
|---|---|---|
| *Blackcurrant Swirl Cheesecake* (Heinz) 1/5 | 241 | 13 |
| *Black Forest Gateau* (Tesco) | 191 | 10 |
| *Bramley Apple Danish* (Sarah Lee) 1/6 | 167 | 4 |
| *Bramley Apple Pies* (Mr Kipling) | 222 | 9 |
| *Carrot Passion Cake* (Entermans) | 208 | 13 |
| *Chocolate Cheesecake* (Heinz Weight Watchers) 1/5 | 297 | 19 |
| *Chocolate Fudge Brownie* (Entermans) | 162 | 2 |
| *Chocolate Fudge Cake* (Entermans) | 127 | 3 |
| *Chocolate Mini Eclairs* (Poppies) | 53 | 4 |
| *Chocolate Mousse* (Heinz Weight Watchers) | 97 | 4 |
| *Chocolate Tiramisu* (Heinz Weight Watchers) | 210 | 4 |
| *Coffee Cake* (Entermans) | 160 | 7 |
| *Coppenwrath Plum Crumble Cake, 1/10, 60g* | 131 | 5 |
| *Cream Horns* (Tesco) | 243 | 16 |
| *Creme Caramel* (Tesco) | 187 | 7 |
| *Custard Danish* (Sarah Lee) 1/6 | 155 | 4 |
| *Custard Slices* (Tesco) | 316 | 16 |
| *Dairy Cream Sponge Sandwich* (Tesco) | 133 | 6 |
| *Deep & Fruity Apple Pie* (Sarah Lee) 1/6 | 260 | 13 |
| *Devonshire Cheese Cake, Blackcurrant 1/6* | 191 | 11 |
| *Devonshire Cheese Cake, Strawberries & Cream 1/6* | 191 | 11 |
| *Double Berry Burst Muffin* (Entermans) | 140 | 2.1 |
| *Finest Chocolate Mousse* (Tesco) per pot | 617 | 44 |

|  | Calories | Fat(g) |
|---|---|---|
| *Finest Fresh Cream Belgium Bun (Tesco)* | 497 | 20 |
| *Finest Jam Roly Poly (Tesco)* | 311 | 11 |
| *Finest Summer Pudding (Tesco)* | 118 | 0.6 |
| *Finest French Apple Tart (Tesco) 1/4* | 210 | 12 |
| *Fresh Cream Slices (Tesco)* | 311 | 209 |
| *Finest Cream Victoria Sponge (Tesco)* | 165 | 8 |
| *Fruit Cocktail Trifle (Tesco) per pot* | 175 | 9 |
| *Go Ahead Chocolate Sundae Sensation (McVities)* | 180 | 3 |
| *Healthy Eating Creamed Rice Pudding (Tesco)* | 136 | 2 |
| *Iced Dessert, Raspberry Swirl (Heinz Weight Watchers)* | 124 | 3 |
| *Iced Dessert, Toffee Flavour & Toffee Sauce (Heinz Weight Watchers)* | 163 | 5 |
| *Iced Dessert, Vanilla & Raspberry Compote (Heinz Weight Watchers)* | 142 | 4 |
| *Iced Dessert, Vanilla & Strawberry Compote (Heinz Weight Watchers)* | 142 | 4 |
| *Illegal Double Chocolate Gateau* | 135 | 6 |
| *Lemon Meringue Pie (Sarah Lee) 1/6* | 202 | 7 |
| *Lemon Torte (Tesco)* | 142 | 6 |
| *Light Chocolate Trifle (Cadbury's)* | 162 | 7 |
| *Lower Fat Cherry Cheese Cake (Tesco)* | 227 | 5 |
| *Lower Fat Manderin Cheese Cake (Tesco)* | 224 | 5 |
| *Low Fat Rice Pudding (Ambrosia)* | 129 | 1.4 |
| *Devon Custard Dessert (Ambrosia) per pot* | 108 | 1.7 |
| *Milk Chocolate Trifle (Cadbury's)* | 276 | 8 |
| *New York Based Cheesecake (Entermans)* | 347 | 21 |

| | Calories | Fat(g) |
|---|---|---|
| *Orange Quick Set Jelly (Rowntree)* | 65 | 0 |
| *Pecan Danish (Sarah Lee) 1/6* | 248 | 13 |
| *Raspberry Cheesecake (Tesco)* | 373 | 28 |
| *Raspberry Danish Twist (Entermans)* | 159 | 2 |
| *Raspberry Quick Set Jelly (Rowntree)* | 65 | 0 |
| *Raspberry Quick Set Sugar Free Jelly (Rowntree) per 2 sachets* | 9 | 0 |
| *Raspberry Sponge Pudding (Tesco)* | 257 | 11 |
| *Raspberry Swirl Cheesecake (Heinz) 1/5* | 231 | 13 |
| *Raspberry Swirl Gateau (Tesco)* | 242 | 14 |
| *Raspberry Trifle (Tesco)* | 140 | 9 |
| *Rhubarb Crumble (Tesco) 1/4* | 312 | 15 |
| *Rice Pudding, No Added Sugar, Low Fat (Heinz Weight Watchers) 1 serving* | 146 | 2.1 |
| *Sarah Lee Double Chocolate Gateau, 1/6* | 192 | 10 |
| *Sponge Pudding, Banoffee Canned (Heinz)* | 307 | 12 |
| *Sponge Pudding, Chocolate with Chocolate Sauce Canned (Heinz)* | 224 | 7 |
| *Sponge Pudding, Chocolate & Cadbury's Chocolate Sauce Canned (Heinz)* | 234 | 9 |
| *Sponge Pudding, Lemon Curd Canned (Heinz)* | 302 | 12 |
| *Sponge Pudding, Spotted Dick Canned (Heinz)* | 243 | 9 |
| *Sponge Pudding, Sticky Toffee Canned (Heinz)* | 235 | 10 |
| *Sponge Pudding, Strawberry Jam Canned (Heinz)* | 338 | 15 |
| *Sponge Pudding, Treacle Canned (Heinz)* | 222 | 6 |

| | Calories | Fat(g) |
|---|---|---|
| *Sticky Toffee Pudding* | 235 | 10 |
| *Strawberry Cheesecake (Heinz), 1/5* | 192 | 10 |
| *Strawberry Flavoured Custard Dessert (Ambrosia) per pot* | 141 | 4 |
| *Strawberry Gateau (Tesco)* | 184 | 11 |
| *Strawberry Pavlova (Tesco)* | 227 | 9 |
| *Strawberry Quick Set Jelly (Rowntree)* | 65 | 0 |
| *Strawberry Quick Set Sugar Free Jelly (Rowntree) per 2 sachets* | 10 | 0 |
| *Strawberry Trifle (Shape St Ivel)* | 168 | 5 |
| *Sugar Free Blackcurrant Quick Set Sugar Free Jelly (Rowntree)* | 37 | 0 |
| *Summer Fruit Pudding (Tesco)* | 72 | 0.2 |
| *Syrup Sponge Pudding (Tesco)* | 380 | 13 |
| *Toffee Chocolate Dessert (Heinz Weight Watchers) per pot* | 178 | 3 |
| *Toffee Flavoured Custard Dessert (Ambrosia) per pot* | 142 | 4 |
| *Toffee Fudge Cake (Entermans)* | 274 | 14 |
| *Traditional Rice Pudding with Sultanas & Nutmeg (Ambrosia) 1/2 tin* | 211 | 6 |

### Pudding Mixes per serving

| | Calories | Fat(g) |
|---|---|---|
| *Banana Flavour Angel Delight with Whole Milk* | 125 | 6 |
| *Banana Flavour Angel Delight with Semi Skimmed Milk* | 111 | 5 |
| *Butterscotch Flavour Angel Delight with Whole Milk* | 108 | 6 |
| *Butterscotch Flavour Angel Delight with Semi Skimmed Milk* | 108 | 4 |
| *Cheese Cake Mix (Tesco)* | 222 | 12 |

| | Calories | Fat (g) |
|---|---|---|
| *Chocolate Blancmange (Pearce Buffs)* | 120 | 2.3 |
| *Chocolate Flavour Angel Delight with Semi Skimmed Milk* | 112 | 4 |
| *Chocolate Flavour Instant Whip with Semi Skimmed Milk (Asda)* | 111 | 4 |
| *Lemon Meringue Crunch (Greens)* | 251 | 9 |
| *No Added Sugar Banana Toffee Flavour Angel Delight* | 495 | 27 |
| *No Added Sugar Butterscotch Flavour Angel Delight with Whole Milk* | 108 | 6 |
| *No Added Sugar Butterscotch Flavour Angel Delight with Semi Skimmed Milk* | 95 | 4 |
| *No Added Sugar Chocolate Flavour Angel Delight with Whole Milk* | 105 | 6 |
| *No Added Sugar Chocolate Flavour Angel Delight with Semi Skimmed Milk* | 92 | 4 |
| *No Added Sugar Vanilla Flavour Delight with Semi Skimmed Milk (Tesco)* | 182 | 7 |
| *No Added Sugar Strawberry Flavour Angel Delight with Semi Skimmed Milk* | 95 | 4 |
| *Pancake Mix (Greens)* | 138 | 2 |
| *Raspberry Flavour Angel Delight with Whole Milk* | 122 | 6 |
| *Raspberry Flavour Angel Delight with Semi Skimmed Milk* | 118 | 5 |
| *Raspberry Flavour Trifle Whip (Birds Eye)* | 205 | 7 |
| *Real Milk Chocolate Dessert with Semi Skimmed Milk (Cadbury's)* | 203 | 7 |

| | Calories | Fat(g) |
|---|---|---|
| *Real Milk Chocolate Orange Flavour Dessert with Semi Skimmed Milk (Cadbury's)* | 125 | 6 |
| *Sponge Mix (McDougalls)* | 138 | 1.4 |
| *Strawberry Blancmange (Pearce Buffs)* | 140 | 5 |
| *Strawberry Flavour Angel Delight with Whole Milk* | 122 | 6 |
| *Strawberry Flavour Angel Delight with Semi Skimmed Milk* | 108 | 4 |
| *Strawberry Flavour Instant Whip with Semi Skimmed Milk (Asda)* | 106 | 4 |
| *Strawberry Flavour Trifle Mix (Birds Eye)* | 205 | 7 |

## PULSES per 100g

**Fat figures are given to the nearest half gram up to three grams and to the nearest gram thereafter**

| | Calories | Fat(g) |
|---|---|---|
| *Chick Peas, boiled* | 120 | 2 |
| *Lentils, boiled* | 100 | 1 |
| *Split Peas, boiled* | 126 | 3 |

## RICE per 100g

| | Calories | Fat(g) |
|---|---|---|
| *American Brown Rice (Safeways)* | 349 | 3 |
| *American Easy Cook Rice (Safeways)* | 375 | 4 |
| *American Long Grain Rice (Safeways)* | 351 | 1 |
| *Arborio Risotto Rice (Tesco)* | 346 | 1 |
| *Basmati Rice* | 345 | 1 |
| *Basmati Rice (Tesco)* | 347 | 1 |

| | Calories | Fat (g) |
|---|---|---|
| *Beef Flavour Savoury Rice* (Batchelors) | 358 | 2 |
| *Boil in the Bag Basmati Rice* (Uncle Ben's) | 343 | 1 |
| *Camargue Red Rice* (Tesco) | 340 | 2 |
| *Chicken Flavour Savoury Rice* (Batchelors) | 354 | 2 |
| *Coriander & Herbs Delicately Flavoured Rice* (Batchelors) | 369 | 4 |
| *Wild Rice* (Tesco) | 354 | 1 |
| *Garlic & Butter Delicately Flavoured Rice* (Batchelors) | 350 | 3 |
| *Golden Savoury Rice* (Batchelors) | 364 | 3 |
| *Italian Arborio Rice* (Safeways) | 349 | 1 |
| *Mild Curry Savoury Rice* (Batchelors) | 355 | 2 |
| *Mushroom Savoury Rice* (Batchelors) | 360 | 2 |
| *Pilau Rice* (Sharwood) | 354 | 1 |
| *Pilau Rice Delicately Flavoured* (Batchelors) | 369 | 4 |
| *Rices of the World Chinese* (Batchelors) | 354 | 2 |
| *Rices of the World Indian* (Batchelors) | 358 | 2 |
| *Rices of the World Spanish* (Batchelors) | 360 | 2 |
| *Rices of the World Sweet & Sour* (Batchelors) | 359 | 2 |
| *Rices of the World Tandoori* (Batchelors) | 358 | 3 |
| *Rices of the World Thai* (Batchelors) | 358 | 2 |
| *Sweetcorn & Peppers Savoury Rice* (Batchelors) | 360 | 2 |
| *Thai Fragrant Rice* (Tesco) | 349 | 0 |
| *Tomato & Herbs Delicately Flavoured Rice* (Batchelors) | 387 | 4 |
| *Valencia Rice, Spanish Paella* (Tesco) | 348 | 1 |

| | Calories | Fat (g) |
|---|---|---|
| *Wholegrain Brown Rice* | 346 | 3 |
| *Wild Rice (Tesco)* | 354 | 1 |

## SANDWICH FILLINGS & SPREADS per 100g

| | Calories | Fat (g) |
|---|---|---|
| *Chicken with Salad Vegetables Sandwich Fillers (Heinz)* | 203 | 15 |
| *Chicken & Mushroom Toast Toppers (Heinz)* | 56 | 1 |
| *Cucumber Sandwich Spread (Heinz)* | 164 | 12 |
| *Ham with Salad Vegetables Sandwich Fillers (Heinz)* | 204 | 16 |
| *Ham & Cheese Toast Toppers (Heinz)* | 96 | 4 |
| *Mild Chicken Tikka & Salad Vegetables Sandwich Fillers (Heinz)* | 196 | 14 |
| *Mushroom & Bacon Toast Toppers (Heinz)* | 94 | 4 |
| *Original Sandwich Spread (Heinz)* | 225 | 13 |
| *Prawn & Salad Vegetables Sandwich Fillers (Heinz)* | 201 | 14 |
| *Tuna & Sweetcorn wih Salad Vegetables Sandwich Fillers (Heinz)* | 191 | 13 |

## SAUCES, CHUTNEYS & RELISHES 25g per tbsp

| | Calories | Fat (g) |
|---|---|---|
| *Apple, Cider & Mustard Sauce (Colman's) per tbsp* | 28 | 0 |
| *Apricot Chutney (Sharwood) per tbsp* | 33 | 0 |
| *Basil & Chilli Stir Fry Sauce (Sharwood) 100g* | 49 | 1 |
| *Bengal Hot Chutney (Sharwood) per tbsp* | 50 | 0 |
| *Black Bean Stir Fry Sauce (Sharwood) 100g* | 93 | 1 |

| | Calories | Fat (g) |
|---|---|---|
| *Bramley Apple Sauce (Colman's) 100g* | 108 | 0 |
| *Chilli & Kaffir Lime Leaf Stir Fry Sauce (Sharwood) 100g* | 106 | 6 |
| *Chop Suey Stir Fry Sauce (Sharwood) 100g* | 75 | 2 |
| *Classic Mint Sauce (Colman's) per tbsp* | 28 | 0 |
| *Cranberry & Orange Sauce with Port (Colman's) 100g* | 274 | 0 |
| *Curried Fruit Chutney (Sharwood) per tbsp* | 32 | 0 |
| *Dijon Mustard (Colman's) per tbsp* | 30 | 3 |
| *Dijonnaise (Hellmann's) per tbsp* | 52 | 20 |
| *Fresh Garden Mint (Colman's) per tbsp* | 6 | 0 |
| *Ginger & Honey Stir Fry Sauce (Sharwood) 100g* | 92 | 0 |
| *Green Label Chutney Dip (Sharwood) per tbsp* | 59 | 0 |
| *Green Label Mango Chutney (Sharwood) per tbsp* | 59 | 0 |
| *Hoi-Sin & Spring Onion Stir Fry Sauce (Sharwood) 100g* | 133 | 2 |
| *Horseradish Relish (Colman's) per tbsp* | 27 | 2 |
| *Hot Chilli Sauce (Sharwood) per tbsp* | 30 | 0 |
| *Lemon & Tarragon Sauce (Colman's) per tbsp* | 72 | 6 |
| *Lemongrass & Coriander Stir Fry Sauce (Sharwood) 100g* | 64 | 2 |
| *Lemongrass & Ginger Stir Fry Sauce (Sharwood) 100g* | 72 | 3 |
| *Light Mayonnaise (Hellmann's) per tbsp* | 75 | 8 |
| *Light Soy Sauce (Sharwood) per tbsp* | 5 | 0 |
| *Lime Indian Pickle (Sharwood) per tbsp* | 38 | 2 |
| *Major Grey Chutney (Sharwood) per tbsp* | 54 | 0 |
| *Mango & Apple Chutney (Sharwood) per tbsp* | 58 | 0 |

|  | Calories | Fat (g) |
|---|---|---|
| *Mango & Lime Chutney (Sharwood) per tbsp* | 52 | 0 |
| *Mediterranean Mayonnaise (Hellmann's) per tbsp* | 181 | 20 |
| *Mild Mustard Pickle (Heinz) per tbsp* | 32 | 0 |
| *Peach Chutney (Sharwood) per tbsp* | 43 | 0 |
| *Peppercorn Mustard (Colman's) per tbsp* | 35 | 1 |
| *Piccalilli Pickle (Heinz) per tbsp* | 27 | 0 |
| *Ploughman's Pickle (Heinz) per tbsp* | 29 | 0 |
| *Real Mayonnaise (Hellmann's) per tbsp* | 181 | 20 |
| *Real Oyster Sauce (Sharwood) per tbsp* | 19 | 0 |
| *Redcurrant (Colman's) per tbsp* | 92 | 0 |
| *Rich Soy Sauce (Sharwood) per tbsp* | 12 | 0 |
| *Salad Cream (Heinz) per tbsp* | 83 | 7 |
| *Salad Cream, Light (Heinz) per tbsp* | 61 | 5 |
| *Seafood Sauce (Colman's) per tbsp* | 51 | 4 |
| *Sweet Chilli Sauce (Sharwood) per tbsp* | 46 | 0 |
| *Sweet & Sour Stir Fry Sauce (Sharwood) 100g* | 25 | 0 |
| *Szechuan Stir Fry Sauce (Sharwood) 100g* | 21 | 1 |
| *Tamarind & Lime Stir Fry Sauce (Sharwood) 100g* | 139 | 5 |
| *Tangy Tomato Pickle (Heinz) per tbsp* | 26 | 0 |
| *Tartare Sauce (Colman's) per tbsp* | 70 | 6 |
| *Teriyaki Stir Fry Sauce (Sharwood) 100g* | 23 | 0 |
| *Tomato Ketchup (Heinz) per tbsp* | 27 | 0 |
| *Wholegrain Mustard (Colman's) per tbsp* | 35 | 1 |

| | Calories | Fat(g) |
|---|---|---|
| *Yellow Bean Stir Fry Sauce (Sharwood) 100g* | *132* | *2* |

## SOUPS – All soups are given per 100mls

Campbells soups are shown per 100mls of ready to serve soup when the soup is diluted with one can of water.

| | Calories | Fat(g) |
|---|---|---|
| *99% Fat Free Chicken Soup (Campbell's)* | *34* | *1* |
| *99% Fat Free Mushroom Soup (Campbell's)* | *24* | *1* |
| *99% Fat Free Tomato Soup (Campbell's)* | *44* | *1* |
| *99% Fat Free Tomato & Red Pepper Soup (Campbell's)* | *42* | *1* |
| *Asparagus & Potato Soup, pouch (Heinz)* | *49* | *3* |
| *Beef Soup (Heinz)* | *41* | *2* |
| *Big Soup, Beef Broth (Heinz)* | *41* | *1* |
| *Big Soup, Beef & Vegetable Soup (Heinz)* | *45* | *1* |
| *Big Soup, Chicken & Ham Soup (Heinz)* | *41* | *1* |
| *Big Soup, Chicken & Leek Soup (Heinz)* | *59* | *2* |
| *Big Soup, Chicken & Pasta Soup (Heinz)* | *34* | *0* |
| *Big Soup, Chicken & Vegetable Soup (Heinz)* | *47* | *1* |
| *Big Soup, Cumberland Sausage Hotpot Soup (Heinz)* | *53* | *2* |
| *Big Soup, Giant Minestrone Soup (Heinz)* | *44* | *1* |
| *Big Soup, Italian Chicken & Pasta Soup (Heinz)* | *55* | *1* |
| *Big Soup, Lamb & Vegetable Soup (Heinz)* | *56* | *1* |
| *Big Soup, Minted Lamb Hotpot Soup (Heinz)* | *51* | *1* |
| *Big Soup, Turkey & Cumberland Sausage Soup (Heinz)* | *48* | *1* |

| | Calories | Fat(g) |
|---|---|---|
| *Big Soup, Vegetable & Ham Soup (Heinz)* | 50 | 0 |
| *Blended Autumn Vegetable Soup (Heinz)* | 57 | 3 |
| *Blended Carrot & Coriander Soup (Heinz)* | 52 | 3 |
| *Blended Leek & Bacon Soup (Heinz)* | 54 | 3 |
| *Blended Mediterranean Tomato & Courgette Soup (Heinz)* | 40 | 2 |
| *Blended Parsnip & Potato Soup (Heinz)* | 57 | 3 |
| *Blended Red Pepper with Tomato Soup (Heinz)* | 51 | 3 |
| *Blended Sweetcorn & Yellow Pepper Soup (Heinz)* | 49 | 2 |
| *Broccoli & Cheddar Soup, Pouch (Heinz)* | 79 | 6 |
| *Carrot Potato & Coriander Soup (Heinz Weight Watchers)* | 25 | 0 |
| *Carrot & Coriander Deliciously Good Soup (Campbell's)* | 44 | 2 |
| *Carrot & Lentil Soup (Heinz Weight Watchers)* | 31 | 0 |
| *Carrot & Orange Soup, pouch (Heinz)* | 60 | 2 |
| *Chicken Noodle Soup (Heinz Weight Watchers)* | 17 | 0 |
| *Chicken Noodle Soup (Heinz)* | 27 | 0 |
| *Chicken Soup (Heinz Weight Watchers)* | 30 | 1 |
| *Chicken & White Wine Soup Special Choice (Campbell's)* | 49 | 3 |
| *Condensed Soup, Cream of Chicken (Heinz)* | 85 | 6 |
| *Condensed Soup, Cream of Mushroom (Heinz)* | 84 | 6 |
| *Condensed Soup, Vegetable (Heinz)* | 49 | 0 |
| *Consomme Special Choice (Campbell's)* | 7 | 0 |
| *Country Vegetable Soup (Heinz Weight Watchers)* | 30 | 0 |
| *Country Vegetable Soup (Heinz)* | 51 | 1 |

| | Calories | Fat (g) |
|---|---|---|
| Cream Of Asparagus Soup Special Choice (Campbell's) | 45 | 3 |
| Cream Of Celery Soup (Campbell's) | 47 | 3 |
| Cream Of Celery Soup (Heinz) | 44 | 3 |
| Cream Of Chicken Ready To Serve Soup (Homepride) | 46 | 3 |
| Cream Of Chicken Soup (Heinz) | 51 | 3 |
| Cream Of Chicken & Mushroom Soup (Heinz) | 49 | 3 |
| Cream Of Mushroom Ready To Serve Soup (Homepride) | 44 | 3 |
| Cream Of Mushroom Soup (Campbell's) | 69 | 5 |
| Cream Of Mushroom Soup (Heinz) | 51 | 3 |
| Cream Of Sweetcorn Soup (Campbell's) | 51 | 3 |
| Cream Of Tomato Ready To Serve Soup (Homepride) | 60 | 3 |
| Cream Of Tomato Soup (Campbell's) | 66 | 3 |
| Cream Of Tomato Soup (Heinz) | 64 | 4 |
| Cream Of Tomato & Red Pepper Soup (Campbell's) | 62 | 3 |
| Forest Mushroom Soup (Heinz) | 43 | 2 |
| Golden Sweetcorn & Chicken Chowder Soup (Heinz) | 54 | 3 |
| Harvest Carrot & Lima Bean Soup (Heinz) | 40 | 1 |
| Hearty Minestrone Soup (Campbell's) | 26 | 0 |
| Lentil Soup (Campbell's) | 27 | 1 |
| Lentil Soup (Heinz) | 39 | 0 |
| Mediterranean Tomato Soup (Campbell's) | 28 | 0 |
| Mediterranean Tomato & Vegetable Soup (Heinz Weight Watchers) | 16 | 0 |

| | Calories | Fat(g) |
|---|---|---|
| *Minestrone Soup* (Heinz Weight Watchers) | 20 | 0 |
| *Minestrone Soup* (Heinz) | 32 | 1 |
| *Mulligatawny Beef Curry Soup* (Heinz) | 60 | 3 |
| *Mushroom Soup* (Heinz Weight Watchers) | 32 | 1 |
| *Mushroom & Herb Deliciously Good Soup* (Campbell's) | 43 | 3 |
| *Oxtail Soup* (Campbell's) | 40 | 2 |
| *Oxtail Soup* (Heinz) | 41 | 1 |
| *Potato & Leek Deliciously Good Soup* (Campbell's) | 44 | 2 |
| *Roast Mediterranean Vegetable Soup* (Heinz) | 32 | 1 |
| *Scotch Broth* (Campbell's) | 41 | 2 |
| *Scottish Vegetable Soup with Lentils & Beef* (Heinz) | 52 | 1 |
| *Spring Vegetable Soup* (Campbell's) | 21 | 0 |
| *Spring Vegetable Soup* (Heinz) | 31 | 0 |
| *Thick Beef Broth* (Heinz) | 48 | 2 |
| *Thick Beef & Vegetable Soup* (Heinz) | 38 | 1 |
| *Thick Chicken & Vegetable Soup* (Heinz) | 38 | 1 |
| *Thick Lamb & Vegetable Soup* (Heinz) | 37 | 1 |
| *Thick Pea & Ham Soup* (Heinz) | 51 | 0 |
| *Thick Potato & Leek Soup* (Heinz) | 34 | 1 |
| *Thick Scotch Broth* (Heinz) | 47 | 1 |
| *Tomato & Red Pepper Ready To Serve Soup* (Homepride) | 52 | 2 |
| *Tomato Onion & Pepper Soup, Pouch* (Heinz) | 62 | 4 |
| *Tomato Soup 90% Fat Free* (Campbell's) | 44 | 1 |

| | Calories | Fat(g) |
|---|---|---|
| Tomato & Herb Deliciously Good Soup (Campbell's) | 36 | 1 |
| Tomato & Lentil Soup (Heinz) | 54 | 0 |
| Vegetable Soup (Campbell's) | 35 | 1 |
| Vegetable Soup (Heinz) | 47 | 1 |
| Winter Vegetable Soup (Heinz) | 46 | 0 |

## DRIED SOUP MIXES per pack

| | Calories | Fat(g) |
|---|---|---|
| Broccoli & Cauliflower Slim a Soup (Batchelors) | 59 | 2 |
| Cajun Spicy Vegetable Slim a Soup (Batchelors) | 59 | 1 |
| Cheese & Broccoli with Tagliatelle Cup a Soup Extra (Batchelors) | 160 | 5 |
| Chicken Vegetable & Noodle Slim a Soup (Batchelors) | 59 | 1 |
| Chicken & Mushroom Slim a Soup (Batchelors) | 59 | 2 |
| Chicken & Mushroom with Pasta Cup a Soup Extra (Batchelors) | 132 | 4 |
| Chicken & Sweetcorn Slim a Soup (Batchelors) | 59 | 2 |
| Chicken & Tarragon Cup a Soup Thick & Creamy (Batchelors) | 118 | 6 |
| Chinese Chicken Noodle Cup a Soup Extra (Batchelors) | 101 | 1 |
| Cream Of Chicken Soup (Knorr) | 119 | 8 |
| Cream Of Mushroom Soup (Knorr) | 114 | 8 |
| Cream Of Tomato Soup (Knorr) | 136 | 7 |
| Crofter's Chicken & Leek Soup (Knorr) | 83 | 5 |
| Crofter's Thick Vegetable Soup (Knorr) | 80 | 3 |
| Florida Spring Vegetable Soup (Knorr) | 35 | 1 |

| | Calories | Fat(g) |
|---|---|---|
| *French Onion Soup* (Knorr) | 39 | 0 |
| *Golden Vegetable Slim a Soup* (Batchelors) | 58 | 2 |
| *Golden Vegetable Soup* (Knorr) | 100 | 5 |
| *Hot & Sour with Noodles & Vegetables Cup a Soup Extra* (Batchelors) | 89 | 1 |
| *Leek & Potato Slim a Soup* (Batchelors) | 57 | 1 |
| *Mediterranean Tomato Slim a Soup* (Batchelors) | 58 | 1 |
| *Minestrone Slim a Soup* (Batchelors) | 53 | 1 |
| *Minestrone Soup* (Knorr) | 59 | 1 |
| *Minestrone with Pasta Cup a Soup Extra* (Batchelors) | 123 | 1 |
| *Spicy Vegetable with Noodle Cup a Soup Extra* (Batchelors) | 109 | 1 |
| *Super Chicken Noodle Soup* (Knorr) | 61 | 1 |
| *Tangy Tomato with Pasta Cup a Soup Extra* (Batchelors) | 132 | 2 |
| *Thai Chicken with Lemongrass Cup a Soup Thick & Creamy* (Batchelors) | 120 | 5 |
| *Tomato & Lentil Slim a Soup* (Batchelors) | 57 | 0 |
| *Woodland Mushroom Cup a Soup Thick & Creamy* (Batchelors) | 123 | 5 |

## STOCK CUBES

| | Calories | Fat(g) |
|---|---|---|
| *Basil Herb Cubes* (Knorr) per cube | 47 | 3 |
| *Beef Stock Cubes* (Knorr) per cube | 33 | 2 |
| *Bovril Beef Extract Drink* (per 100g) | 183 | 5 |
| *Bovril Chicken Savoury Drink* (per 100g) | 133 | 2 |

| | Calories | Fat(g) |
|---|---|---|
| *Bovril Stock Cube per cube* | 12 | 0 |
| *Chicken Gravy Granules (Oxo, per 100g)* | 305 | 5 |
| *Chicken Oxo Cubes per cube* | 15 | 0 |
| *Chicken Stock Cubes (Knorr) per cube* | 30 | 2 |
| *Chinese - Herb & Spice Cubes (Brooke Bond, per 100g)* | 263 | 6 |
| *Fish Stock Cubes (Knorr) per cube* | 32 | 2 |
| *Garlic & Italian Herbs Seasoning Cubes for Pasta (Knorr) per cube* | 28 | 2 |
| *Indian - Herb & Spice Cubes (Brooke Bond, per 100g)* | 291 | 8 |
| *Italian - Herb & Spice Cubes (Brooke Bond, per 100g)* | 309 | 7 |
| *Lamb Oxo Cubes per cube* | 19 | 0 |
| *Lamb Stock Cubes per cube (Knorr)* | 30 | 2 |
| *Mixed Herbs – Basil & Thyme (Knorr) per cube* | 47 | 3 |
| *Mixed Herb Cubes (Knorr) per cube* | 37 | 3 |
| *Oriental Spices Seasoning Cubes for Stir Fry (Knorr) per cube* | 41 | 3 |
| *Original Gravy Granules (Oxo, per 100g)* | 313 | 5 |
| *Original Oxo Cubes per cube* | 17 | 0 |
| *Parsley & Garlic Herb Cubes (Knorr) per cube* | 42 | 3 |
| *Pilau Seasoning Cubes for Rice (Knorr) per cube* | 30 | 2 |
| *Pork Stock Cubes (Knorr) per cube* | 34 | 3 |
| *Saffron Seasoning Cubes for Rice (Knorr) per cube* | 29 | 2 |
| *Vegetable Gravy Granules (Oxo, per 100g)* | 316 | 5 |
| *Vegetable Oxo Cubes per cube* | 17 | 0 |

| | Calories | Fat (g) |
|---|---|---|
| *Vegetable Stock Cubes (Knorr) per cube* | 31 | 2 |

## SYRUPS & CUSTARDS – per tablespoon (approx)

| | | |
|---|---|---|
| *Chocolate Nut Spread* | 143 | 10 |
| *Custard, canned* | 25 | .1 |
| *Custard, home made with Skimmed Milk* | 20 | .0 |
| *Devon Custard (Ambrosia)* | 26 | .1 |
| *Devon Custard, low fat (Ambrosia)* | 18 | 0 |
| *Golden Syrup* | 78 | 0 |

## TINNED FRUIT per 100g

| | | |
|---|---|---|
| *Apple Slices (John West)* | 20 | 0 |
| *Apricots in Fruit Juice (John West)* | 38 | 0 |
| *Apricots in Syrup* | 59 | 0 |
| *Blackberries in Fruit Juice (John West)* | 39 | 0 |
| *Black Cherries in Syrup* | 70 | 0 |
| *Fruit Cocktail in Juice* | 33 | 0 |
| *Fruit Cocktail in Syrup* | 62 | 0 |
| *Grapefruit in Syrup* | 62 | 0 |
| *Grapefruit Segments in Grapefruit Juice (John West)* | 36 | 0 |
| *Lychees in Syrup* | 68 | 0 |
| *Mandarin Oranges in Syrup* | 62 | 0 |
| *Mandarin Orange Segments in Natural Juice (John West)* | 43 | 0 |

| | Calories | Fat (g) |
|---|---|---|
| *Mangoes in Syrup* | 77 | 0 |
| *Peaches in Fruit Juice (John West)* | 38 | 0 |
| *Peaches in Juice* | 38 | 0 |
| *Peaches in Syrup* | 68 | 0 |
| *Pears in Juice* | 37 | 0 |
| *Pears in Syrup* | 64 | 0 |
| *Pineapple Rings in Pineapple Juice (John West)* | 44 | 0 |
| *Pineapple in Juice* | 54 | 0 |
| *Pineapple in Syrup* | 68 | 0 |
| *Prunes in Fruit Juice (John West)* | 68 | 0 |
| *Raspberries in Fruit Juice (John West)* | 27 | 0 |
| *Raspberries in syrup* | 82 | 0 |
| *Red Cherries in Syrup (John West)* | 70 | 0 |
| *Red Plums in Syrup* | 83 | 0 |
| *Strawberries in Fruit Juice (John West)* | 38 | 0 |
| *Summer Fruits in Syrup (John West)* | 69 | 0 |

## TINNED FISH per 100g

| | Calories | Fat (g) |
|---|---|---|
| *Anchovies in Olive Oil (John West)* | 226 | 14 |
| *Baby Clams in Brine (John West)* | 38 | 0.3 |
| *Dressed Crab (John West)* | 143 | 7 |
| *Dressed Lobster (John West)* | 45 | 5 |
| *Herring Fillets in Horseradish Sauce (John West)* | 230 | 18 |

| | Calories | Fat (g) |
|---|---|---|
| *Herring Fillets in Mustard & Dill Sauce (John West)* | 224 | 18 |
| *Herring Fillets in Tomato Sauce (John West)* | 219 | 17 |
| *Keta Salmon (John West)* | 141 | 5 |
| *Kipper Fillets in Brine (John West)* | 192 | 12 |
| *Kipper Fillets in Sunflower Oil (John West)* | 229 | 17 |
| *Lumpfish Caviar (John West)* | 92 | 4 |
| *Mackerel Fillets in Brine (John West)* | 233 | 17 |
| *Mackerel Fillets in Curry Sauce (John West)* | 233 | 17 |
| *Mackerel Fillets in Green Peppercorn Sauce (John West)* | 263 | 21 |
| *Mackerel Fillets in Mustard Sauce (John West)* | 215 | 15 |
| *Mackerel Fillets in Spicy Tomato Sauce (John West)* | 214 | 14 |
| *Mackerel Fillets in Sunflower Oil (John West)* | 260 | 20 |
| *Mackerel Fillets in Tomato Sauce (John West)* | 213 | 15 |
| *Mackerel Steak in Brine (John West)* | 243 | 19 |
| *Mackerel Steak in Tomato Sauce (John West)* | 221 | 17 |
| *Medium Red Salmon (John West)* | 160 | 8 |
| *Pilchards in Tomato Sauce (John West)* | 123 | 5 |
| *Pink Salmon (John West)* | 155 | 7 |
| *Pink Salmon (Princes)* | 124 | 6 |
| *Pink Salmon, Low Salt (John West)* | 143 | 7 |
| *Pink Salmon, Skinless & Boneless (John West)* | 124 | 4 |
| *Pink Salmon, Smoked (John West)* | 155 | 7 |
| *Prawns in Brine (John West)* | 97 | 1 |

| | Calories | Fat (g) |
|---|---|---|
| *Red Salmon (John West)* | 168 | 8 |
| *Red Salmon, Low Salt (John West)* | 168 | 8 |
| *Red Salmon, Skinless & Boneless (John West)* | 168 | 8 |
| *Tuna Chunks in Brine (John West)* | 113 | 1 |
| *Tuna Chunks in Springwater (John West)* | 113 | 1 |
| *Tuna Chunks in Sunflower Oil (John West)* | 189 | 9 |

## TINNED MEAT per 100g

| | Calories | Fat (g) |
|---|---|---|
| *Canned Beef* | 112 | 4 |
| *Luncheon Meat* | 316 | 26 |

## TINNED VEGETABLES, BEANS & PASTA per 100g

### Vegetables

| | Calories | Fat (g) |
|---|---|---|
| *Asparagus Spears (Green Giant)* | 16 | 0 |
| *Beansprouts* | 31 | 0 |
| *Borlotti Beans* | 103 | 0 |
| *Broad Beans* | 81 | 1 |
| *Butter Beans* | 77 | 1 |
| *Butter Beans (Batchelors)* | 83 | 0 |
| *Cannellini Beans* | 110 | 1 |
| *Carrots* | 20 | 0 |
| *Chick Peas* | 115 | 3 |
| *Chilli Beans* | 116 | 1 |

| | Calories | Fat(g) |
|---|---|---|
| *Chilli Beans in Sauce (Batchelors)* | 101 | 0 |
| *Flageolet Beans* | 103 | 1 |
| *Green Beans* | 24 | 0 |
| *Mushrooms* | 12 | 0 |
| *Mushy Peas (Batchelors)* | 77 | 0 |
| *New Potatoes (John West)* | 64 | 0 |
| *Peas* | 79 | 2 |
| *Peas, Marrowfat* | 100 | 1 |
| *Peas, Mushy* | 81 | 1 |
| *Peas, Processed* | 99 | 1 |
| *Ratatouille (John West)* | 42 | 1 |
| *Red Kidney Beans* | 100 | 1 |
| *Red Kidney Beans (Batchelors)* | 91 | 1 |
| *Sweetcorn in Brine (John West)* | 107 | 0 |
| *Sweetcorn, kernels* | 122 | 1 |
| *Tomatoes* | 17 | 0 |
| *Tomatoes, peeled plum* | 16 | 0 |

## Baked Beans per 100g

| | Calories | Fat(g) |
|---|---|---|
| *Baked Beans in Tomato Sauce (Heinz Weight Watchers)* | 66 | 0 |
| *Baked Beans in Tomato Sauce (Heinz)* | 81 | 0 |
| *Baked Beans in Tomato Sauce (Tesco)* | 85 | 0 |
| *Baked Beans with Bacon (Heinz)* | 91 | 2 |

| | Calories | Fat(g) |
|---|---|---|
| *Baked Beans with Chicken Nuggets (Heinz)* | 105 | 3 |
| *Baked Beans with Pork Sausages (Heinz)* | 89 | 3 |
| *Baked Beans with Vegetable Sausages (Heinz)* | 106 | 4 |
| *Barbecue Beans (Heinz)* | 82 | 0 |
| *Curried Beans (Heinz)* | 103 | 1 |
| *Healthy Balance, Baked Beans in Tomato Sauce (Heinz)* | 67 | 0 |
| *Healthy Balance, Baked Beans with Vegetable Sausages (Heinz)* | 99 | 4 |
| *Value Baked Beans in Tomato Sauce (Tesco)* | 78 | 0 |

### Tinned Pasta per 100g

| | Calories | Fat(g) |
|---|---|---|
| *Bill & Ben, Pasta Shapes in Tomato Sauce (Heinz)* | 61 | 0 |
| *Barbie, Pasta Shapes in Tomato Sauce (Heinz)* | 60 | 0 |
| *Cheese & Tomato Ravioli in Tomato Sauce (Heinz)* | 81 | 2 |
| *Chicken Ravioli in a Spicy Indian Sauce (Heinz)* | 83 | 2 |
| *Italiana, Bolognese Shells (Heinz Weight Watchers)* | 72 | 1 |
| *Italiana, Tortellini (Heinz Weight Watchers)* | 60 | 2 |
| *Italiana, Tuna Twists (Heinz Weight Watchers)* | 62 | 1 |
| *Italiana, Vegetable Ravioli in Tomato Sauce (Heinz Weight Watchers)* | 69 | 2 |
| *Macaroni Cheese (Heinz)* | 95 | 5 |
| *Meat Free Ravioli in Tomato Sauce (Heinz)* | 75 | 1 |
| *Meat Free Spaghetti Bolognese (Heinz)* | 80 | 2 |
| *Noddy, Pasta Shapes in Tomato Sauce (Heinz)* | 62 | 0 |

| | Calories | Fat (g) |
|---|---|---|
| *Pasta Shells with Tuna & Sweetcorn in Tomato Sauce (Heinz)* | 79 | 2 |
| *Ravioli in Tomato Sauce (Heinz)* | 73 | 1 |
| *Rugrats, Pasta Shapes in Tomato Sauce (Heinz)* | 61 | 0 |
| *Spaghetti Bolognese (Heinz)* | 86 | 2 |
| *Spaghetti Hoops 'n' Hotdogs in a Smoky Bacon Sauce (Heinz)* | 76 | 2 |
| *Spaghetti Hoops in Tomato Sauce (Heinz)* | 56 | 0 |
| *Spaghetti in Tomato Sauce with Parsley (Heinz Weight Watchers)* | 49 | 0 |
| *Spaghetti in Tomato Sauce (Heinz)* | 61 | 0 |
| *Spaghetti with Chicken Meatballs in Tomato Sauce (Heinz)* | 88 | 3 |
| *Spaghetti with Sausages in Tomato Sauce (Heinz)* | 82 | 3 |
| *Star Wars, Pasta Shapes in Tomato Sauce (Heinz)* | 59 | 0 |
| *Teletubbies, Pasta Shapes in Tomato Sauce (Heinz)* | 61 | 0 |
| *Teletubbies, Pasta Shapes & Mini Sausages (Heinz)* | 91 | 3 |
| *Thomas the Tank Engine, Pasta Shapes in Tomato Sauce (Heinz)* | 59 | 0 |
| *Thomas the Tank Engine, Pasta Shapes & Mini Sausages (Heinz)* | 92 | 3 |
| *Tweenies, Pasta Shapes in Tomato Sauce (Heinz)* | 59 | 0 |

Calories  Fat (g)

## VEGETABLES per 100g

Fat figures are given to the nearest half gram up to three grams
and to the nearest gram thereafter

| | Calories | Fat (g) |
|---|---|---|
| Artichoke, Jerusalem | 47 | 0 |
| Asparagus, cooked | 21 | 0 |
| Aubergine sliced, fried | 302 | 32 |
| Avocado | 134 | 14 |
| Beansprouts, raw | 31 | 0.5 |
| Beansprouts, stir fried | 72 | 6 |
| Beetroot, raw | 36 | 0 |
| Broad Beans, boiled | 81 | 1 |
| Broccoli, boiled | 24 | 1 |
| Butter Beans, boiled | 103 | 1 |
| Cabbage, boiled | 18 | 1 |
| Cabbage, raw | 26 | 0 |
| Carrots, boiled | 23 | 0 |
| Carrots, raw | 35 | 0 |
| Cauliflower, boiled | 28 | 1 |
| Cauliflower, raw | 34 | 1 |
| Celeriac, boiled | 15 | 1 |
| Celeriac, raw | 18 | 0 |
| Celery, boiled | 8 | 0 |
| Celery, raw | 7 | 0 |

| | Calories | Fat (g) |
|---|---|---|
| *Chicory, raw* | 11 | 1 |
| *Corn on the Cob, boiled* | 66 | 1 |
| *Courgettes, boiled* | 19 | 0 |
| *Courgettes, fried* | 63 | 5 |
| *Cucumber* | 9 | 0 |
| *Curly Kale, boiled* | 24 | 1 |
| *Fennel* | 11 | 0 |
| *Green Beans, boiled* | 25 | 0 |
| *Leeks, boiled* | 21 | 1 |
| *Lettuce* | 14 | 1 |
| *Mange Tout, boiled* | 26 | 0 |
| *Mange Tout, stir fried* | 71 | 5 |
| *Marrow, boiled* | 9 | 0 |
| *Mushrooms, fried in butter* | 157 | 16 |
| *Mushrooms, oyster* | 8 | 0 |
| *Mushrooms, raw* | 13 | 1 |
| *Mushrooms, shiitake, cooked* | 55 | 0 |
| *Okra, boiled* | 28 | 1 |
| *Okra, stir-fried* | 269 | 26 |
| *Onions, fried* | 164 | 11 |
| *Onions, pickled* | 24 | 0 |
| *Onions, raw* | 36 | 0 |
| *Parsnip, boiled* | 66 | 1 |

|  | Calories | Fat (g) |
|---|---|---|
| Peas, boiled | 79 | 2 |
| Peppers, green, raw | 15 | 0 |
| Peppers, red raw | 32 | 0 |
| Peppers, yellow, raw | 26 | 0 |
| Potatoes, new, boiled in skins | 66 | 0 |
| Potatoes, old, baked | 136 | 0 |
| Potatoes, old, boiled | 72 | 0 |
| Potatoes, old, mashed with butter | 104 | 4 |
| Potatoes, old, roast in oil | 149 | 5 |
| Radiccio | 14 | 0 |
| Radish | 12 | 0 |
| Runner Beans, boiled | 18 | 1 |
| Spinach, boiled | 19 | 1 |
| Spinach, raw | 25 | 1 |
| Spring Greens, boiled | 20 | 1 |
| Spring Onions | 23 | 1 |
| Swede, boiled | 11 | 0 |
| Sweet Potato, boiled | 84 | 1 |
| Tomatoes, fried | 91 | 8 |
| Tomatoes, grilled | 49 | 1 |
| Tomatoes, raw | 17 | 0 |
| Turnips, boiled | 12 | 0 |

Calories Fat(g)

## YOGHURTS per tub

| | Calories | Fat(g) |
|---|---|---|
| *Benecol Low Fat Bio Yoghurt, Apricot* | 98 | 0.8 |
| *Benecol Low Fat Bio Yoghurt, Cherry* | 101 | 0.8 |
| *Benecol Low Fat Bio Yoghurt, Raspberry* | 99 | 0.8 |
| *Benecol Low Fat Bio Yoghurt, Strawberry* | 98 | 0.8 |
| *Danone Bio Activa Yoghurt with Prunes, per 100g* | 99 | 2.8 |
| *Danone Bio Activa Yoghurt with Cereal, per 100g* | 98 | 2.8 |
| *Danone Bio Activa 0% Fat, Peaches per, 100g* | 51 | 0.1 |
| *Danone Bio Activa 0% Fat, Red Cherries, per 100g* | 52 | 0.1 |
| *Danone Bio Activa Yoghurt with Cereal, per 100g* | 98 | 2.8 |
| *Heinz Weight Watchers' Yoghurts, Low Fat Yoplait, Black Cherry* | 55 | 0.1 |
| *Heinz Weight Watchers' Yoghurts, Low Fat Yoplait, Peach* | 52 | 0.1 |
| *Heinz Weight Watchers' Yoghurts, Low Fat Yoplait, Raspberry* | 49 | 0.2 |
| *Heinz Weight Watchers' Yoghurts, Low Fat Yoplait, Strawberry* | 52 | 0.1 |
| *Heinz Weight Watchers' Yoghurts, Low Fat Yoplait, Toffee* | 52 | 0.1 |
| *Heinz Weight Watchers' Yoghurts, Low Fat Yoplait, Vanilla* | 50 | 0.1 |
| *Muller Fruit Corner, Blackberry & Raspberry* | 193 | 6.8 |
| *Muller Fruit Corner, Blueberry* | 196 | 6.8 |
| *Muller Fruit Corner, Peach & Apricot* | 193 | 6.8 |
| *Muller Fruit Corner, Red Cherries* | 193 | 6.8 |
| *Muller Fruit Corner, Strawberry* | 206 | 6.8 |
| *Muller Light Yoghurt, Banana* | 106 | 0.2 |
| *Muller Light Yoghurt, Cherry* | 100 | 0.2 |

| | Calories | Fat(g) |
|---|---|---|
| *Muller Light Yoghurt, Chocolate* | 108 | 0.6 |
| *Muller Light Yoghurt, Country Berries* | 104 | 0.2 |
| *Muller Light Yoghurt, Lemon & Lime* | 106 | 0.2 |
| *Muller Light Yoghurt, Pineapple & Peach* | 106 | 0.2 |
| *Muller Light Yoghurt, Strawberry* | 106 | 0.2 |
| *Muller Light Yoghurt, Toffee* | 106 | 0.2 |
| *Shape Fat Free Bio Yoghurt, Black Cherry & Raspberry (St Ivel)* | 53 | 0.2 |
| *Shape Fat Free Bio Yoghurt, Cranberry & Blackberry (St Ivel)* | 54 | 0.2 |
| *Shape Fat Free Bio Yoghurt, Red Cherry (St Ivel)* | 57 | 0.2 |
| *Shape Fat Free Bio Yoghurt, Strawberry (St Ivel)* | 56 | 0.2 |
| *Ski Low Fat Yoghurt, Apricot & Mango* | 127 | 2.3 |
| *Ski Low Fat Yoghurt, Blackcherry* | 130 | 2.3 |
| *Ski Low Fat Yoghurt, Lemon* | 130 | 2.5 |
| *Ski Low Fat Yoghurt, Orange & Guava* | 128 | 2.4 |
| *Ski Low Fat Yoghurt, Passionfruit & Peach* | 129 | 2.4 |
| *Ski Low Fat Yoghurt, Pineapple & Grapefruit* | 127 | 2.3 |
| *Ski Low Fat Yoghurt, Raspberry* | 125 | 2.4 |
| *Ski Light Yoghurt Virtually Fat Free, Blackberry & Raspberry* | 67 | 0.3 |
| *Ski Light Yoghurt Virtually Fat Free, Peach & Pineapple* | 70 | 0.1 |
| *Ski Light Yoghurt Virtually Fat Free, Red Cherry* | 61 | 0.3 |
| *Ski Light Yoghurt Virtually Fat Free, Strawberry* | 61 | 0.3 |

|  | Calories | Fat (g) |
|---|---|---|
| **Fromage Frais per tub** | | |
| *Fromage frais, fruit per 100g* | 131 | 6 |
| *Fromage frais, low fat per 100g* | 58 | 0 |
| *Fromage frais, plain per 100g* | 113 | 7 |
| *Tesco Dessert Range, Cherries & Chocolate* | 299 | 15 |
| *Tesco Dessert Range, Chocolate Heaven* | 396 | 31 |
| *Tesco Dessert Range, Rainforest Bliss* | 279 | 13 |
| *Tesco, Natural* | 207 | 0.9 |
| *Yoplait, Apricot, Mango & Vanilla* | 122 | 2 |
| *Yoplait, Blackberry, Apple & Vanilla* | 126 | 2 |
| *Yoplait, Blackcherry* | 134 | 2 |
| *Yoplait, Nectarine, Orange & Vanilla* | 123 | 2 |
| *Yoplait, Peach & Apricot* | 127 | 2 |
| *Yoplait, Strawberry & Vanilla* | 123 | 2 |
| *Yoplait, Summer Fruits* | 128 | 2 |
| | | |
| **Other Desserts per tub** | | |
| *Chocolate Brownie Sundae (Tesco)* | 564 | 58 |
| *Flake Twinpot (Cadbury's)* | 266 | 14 |
| *Fruit Cocktail Trifle (Tesco)* | 175 | 9 |
| *Light Chocolate Mousse (Cadbury's)* | 68 | 2 |
| *Mousse Original (Cadbury's)* | 192 | 7 |
| *Muller Strawberry Crumble* | 222 | 8 |

| | Calories | Fat (g) |
|---|---|---|
| *Muller Mississippi Mud Pie* | 254 | 8 |
| *Muller Rhubarb Crumble* | 222 | 8 |
| *Onken Lite Lemon Mousse* | 156 | 2.3 |
| *Onken Peach Mousse* | 215 | 10 |
| *Onken Strawberry Mousse* | 212 | 10 |
| *Peach Melba Sundae (Tesco)* | 261 | 14 |
| *Shapers Lemon & Lime Yoghurt Mousse* | 88 | 4 |
| *Shapers Strawberry Yoghurt Mousse* | 89 | 4 |
| *Shape Trifle, Mango & Passion Fruit* | 117 | 5 |
| *Shape Trifle, Strawberry* | 168 | 5 |
| *Strawberry Cheesecake (Tesco)* | 254 | 12 |
| *Strawberry Trifle (Tesco)* | 141 | 9 |
| *Trifle (Cadbury's)* | 276 | 18 |

# EATING OUT

It can be hard eating out on a diet. Suddenly you're no longer in control of the menu and you're wide open to temptation. At Slim•Fast, we appreciate that eating out is part of daily life, and because we created the Plan to fit into your life, not the other way round, eating out is still on the menu. This section should help you to make sensible choices when eating out with friends and family.

www.slimfast.co.uk

| | Calories | Fat(g) |
|---|---|---|

## BURGER KING – All per serving

### Breakfast

| | Calories | Fat(g) |
|---|---|---|
| *Sausage & Egg* | 375 | 19 |
| *Bacon & Egg* | 296 | 13 |
| *Sausage, Bacon & Egg* | 430 | 23 |
| *Egg & Cheese* | 282 | 12 |
| *Hash Browns Medium* | 212 | 13 |
| *Hash Browns Large* | 318 | 20 |

### Meals per serving

| | Calories | Fat(g) |
|---|---|---|
| *Whopper* | 646 | 38 |
| *Whopper with Cheese* | 728 | 45 |
| *Double Whopper* | 873 | 54 |
| *Double Whopper with Cheese* | 955 | 60 |
| *Whopper Junior* | 372 | 19 |
| *Whopper Junior with Cheese* | 413 | 23 |
| *Hamburger* | 290 | 10 |
| *Cheeseburger* | 331 | 15 |
| *Double Cheeseburger* | 492 | 26 |
| *Double Cheeseburger with Bacon* | 509 | 28 |
| *BK Big King* | 540 | 31 |
| *BK Chicken Flamer* | 308 | 12 |
| *Chicken Royale* | 638 | 40 |

| | Calories | Fat(g) |
|---|---|---|
| Chicken Royale Strips (4) | 171 | 9 |
| Chicken Royale Strips (6) | 256 | 14 |
| Chicken Whopper | 548 | 23 |
| Chicken Caesar Deli Wrap | 835 | 26 |
| BK Spicy Beanburger | 505 | 20 |
| BK Veggie Whopper | 432 | 17 |
| Fish Pick 'em Ups (4) | 198 | 9 |
| Fish Pick 'em Ups (6) | 298 | 13 |
| King Fries, small | 259 | 11 |
| King Fries, regular | 400 | 16 |
| King Fries, large | 490 | 20 |
| Onion Rings, regular | 261 | 13 |
| Onion Rings, large | 348 | 18 |
| Ketchup Pot | 27 | 0 |
| Ketchup Sachet | 16 | 0 |
| BBQ Sauce Pot | 32 | 0 |

### Desserts per serving

| | | |
|---|---|---|
| Apple Fritters | 157 | 15 |
| Cinnamon Hot Bakes | 399 | 4 |
| Choc Chip Cookie | 79 | 9 |
| Diddy Donuts | 323 | 15 |
| Ice Cream Sundae, Caramel | 189 | 12 |

| | Calories | Fat (g) |
|---|---|---|
| *Ice Cream Sundae, Chocolate* | 189 | 10 |
| *Soft Serve Ice Cream* | 112 | 15 |

### Drinks per serving

| | | |
|---|---|---|
| *Coca Cola, large* | 258 | 0 |
| *Coca Cola, regular* | 172 | 0 |
| *Coca Cola, small* | 129 | 0 |
| *Coffee, white no sugar* | 22 | 4 |
| *Diet Coke, large* | 6 | 0 |
| *Diet Coke, regular* | 4 | 0 |
| *Diet Coke, small* | 3 | 0 |
| *Fanta Orange, large* | 258 | 0 |
| *Fanta Orange, regular* | 172 | 0 |
| *Fanta Orange, small* | 129 | 0 |
| *Hot Chocolate* | 65 | 2 |
| *Milk* | 195 | 7 |
| *Milk Shake, Small Banana* | 217 | 4 |
| *Milk Shake, Small Chocolate* | 226 | 4 |
| *Milk Shake, Small Strawberry* | 212 | 4 |
| *Milk Shake, Small Vanilla* | 176 | 4 |
| *Orange Juice* | 120 | 0 |
| *Sprite, large* | 258 | 0 |
| *Sprite, regular* | 172 | 0 |

| | Calories | Fat (g) |
|---|---|---|
| *Sprite, small* | 128 | 0 |
| *Tea, white no sugar* | 18 | 4 |

## CARVERY – Typical values per serving

Fat figures are given to the nearest half gram up to three grams
and to the nearest gram thereafter

### Starters per serving

| | Calories | Fat (g) |
|---|---|---|
| *Avocado with Prawns* | 340 | 26 |
| *Melon 1/2 Cantaloupe* | 54 | 0 |
| *Pâté on Toast* | 184 | 10 |
| *Prawn Cocktail* | 124 | 12 |
| *Vegetable soup* | 54 | 1 |
| *Cream of tomato soup* | 80 | 5 |

### Main Courses per serving

| | Calories | Fat (g) |
|---|---|---|
| *Bacon roll* | 67 | 5 |
| *Pork crackling 25g* | 138 | 11 |
| *Potatoes, roast* | 204 | 6 |
| *Potatoes, boiled* | 120 | 0 |
| *Roast Beef, lean* | 133 | 4 |
| *Roast Chicken, no skin* | 121 | 3 |
| *Roast Lamb, leg lean* | 162 | 7 |
| *Roast Pork, leg lean* | 157 | 6 |

| | Calories | Fat (g) |
|---|---|---|
| *Turkey, no skin* | 112 | 1 |
| *Yorkshire Pudding* | 104 | 6 |

### Sauces per serving

| | | |
|---|---|---|
| *Apple sauce* | 26 | 0 |
| *Gravy* | 87 | 8 |
| *Horseradish Sauce* | 49 | 5 |
| *Mint Sauce* | 13 | 0 |

### Desserts per serving

| | | |
|---|---|---|
| *Cheesecake* | 242 | 11 |
| *Creme Caramel* | 113 | 3 |
| *Fresh Fruit Salad* | 98 | 0 |
| *Ice Cream, dairy vanilla* | 146 | 7 |
| *Sherry Trifle* | 291 | 16 |

## CHINESE – Typical values per serving

### Starters per serving

| | | |
|---|---|---|
| *Crab Meat & Sweetcorn Soup* | 150 | 3 |
| *Prawn Crackers, each* | 15 | 1 |
| *Spare Ribs, 100g* | 292 | 20 |
| *Spring Rolls, each* | 120 | 6 |

| | Calories | Fat (g) |
|---|---|---|
| **Main Courses** per serving | | |
| *Beef in Oyster Sauce* | 350 | 18 |
| *Chicken & Cashew Nuts* | 400 | 20 |
| *Chicken Chop Suey* | 420 | 15 |
| *Chicken Chow Mein with Noodles* | 650 | 14 |
| *Chicken in Black Bean Sauce* | 300 | 10 |
| *Chilli Crispy Beef* | 650 | 14 |
| *Egg Fu Yung* | 750 | 24 |
| *Fried Rice* | 540 | 16 |
| *Prawn Chop Suey* | 320 | 12 |
| *Shredded Beef* | 530 | 24 |
| *Sweet & Sour Pork* | 850 | 42 |
| *Sweet & Sour Prawns* | 460 | 23 |
| | | |
| **Desserts** per serving | | |
| *Apple fritter, each* | 60 | 4 |
| *Banana fritter, each* | 50 | 4 |

## FISH & CHIP SHOPS – Typical values per serving

| | Calories | Fat (g) |
|---|---|---|
| *Cod in batter* | 320 | 16 |
| *Haddock in batter* | 350 | 16 |
| *Plaice in batter* | 550 | 15 |
| *Rockfish in batter* | 543 | 39 |

| | Calories | Fat (g) |
|---|---|---|
| *Roe in batter* | 200 | 28 |
| *Scampi in batter* | 253 | 14 |
| *Saveloy, each* | 197 | 15 |
| *Chips, small portion* | 400 | 20 |
| *Chips, medium portion 265g* | 670 | 29 |
| *Chips, large portion* | 850 | 42 |
| *Mushy peas* | 80 | 0 |
| *Tartare sauce* | 37 | 3 |
| *Tomato ketchup* | 20 | 0 |

## FRENCH – Typical values per serving

### Starters per serving

| | | |
|---|---|---|
| *French Onion Soup* | 79 | 4 |
| *Coquille St Jacques* | 350 | 5 |

### Main Courses per serving

| | | |
|---|---|---|
| *Beef Bourguignon* | 550 | 25 |
| *Coq au Vin* | 650 | 20 |
| *Moules Mariniere* | 380 | 10 |
| *Sole Veronique* | 550 | 15 |
| *Steak au Poivre* | 480 | 18 |
| *Tornados Rossini* | 600 | 27 |

| | Calories | Fat(g) |
|---|---|---|

## Desserts per serving

| | Calories | Fat(g) |
|---|---|---|
| *Chocolate Gateau* | 400 | 25 |
| *Chocolate Mousse* | 260 | 18 |
| *Crepes Suzette* | 400 | 15 |

## GREEK – Typical values per serving

### Starters per serving

| | Calories | Fat(g) |
|---|---|---|
| *Bean Soup* | 250 | 10 |
| *Greek Salad* | 180 | 8 |
| *Humous with Pitta Bread* | 450 | 20 |
| *Taramasalata with Pitta Bread* | 450 | 20 |
| *Tzatziki with Pitta Bread* | 250 | 15 |

## Main Courses per serving

| | Calories | Fat(g) |
|---|---|---|
| *Kalamari, deep fried* | 500 | 28 |
| *Kalamari, marinated* | 200 | 15 |
| *Kebabs* | 350 | 24 |
| *Meatballs* | 580 | 35 |
| *Moussaka* | 660 | 45 |
| *Stifado* | 560 | 35 |
| *Stuffed Vine Leaves* | 300 | 23 |

| | Calories | Fat (g) |
|---|---|---|

**Desserts per serving**

*Halva* ............................................... 250   21

**INDIAN** – Typical values per serving

**Starters per serving**

*Chapati, each* .................................... 140   12
*Onion Bhaji, each* .............................. 250   12
*Poppadum, each* ................................ 75   4
*Samosa* ............................................. 270   28

**Main Courses per serving**

*Chicken Balti* ..................................... 650   35
*Chicken Dhansak* .............................. 500   52
*Chicken Jalfrezi* ................................ 500   20
*Chicken Korma* .................................. 860   60
*Chicken Madras* ................................ 560   38
*Chicken Tikka Masala* ....................... 600   40
*Chicken Vindaloo* .............................. 500   30
*Lamb Biriyani* .................................... 900   54
*Lamb Roghan Josh* ........................... 700   35
*Prawn Biriyani* .................................. 850   43
*Tandoori Chicken* .............................. 350   23
*Boiled Rice* ....................................... 300   3

| | Calories | Fat (g) |
|---|---|---|
| Naan Bread, each | 300 | 27 |
| Pilau Rice | 450 | 8 |

## ITALIAN – Typical values per serving

### Starters per serving

| | | |
|---|---|---|
| Parma Ham with Figs | 120 | 3 |
| Parma Ham with Melon | 150 | 3 |
| Straciatelle | 100 | 5 |

### Main Courses per serving

| | | |
|---|---|---|
| Cannelloni | 550 | 38 |
| Frito Misto | 1000 | 55 |
| Lasagne | 650 | 45 |
| Pasta Con Porcini | 600 | 22 |
| Ravioli | 520 | 28 |
| Spaghetti Bolognese | 720 | 35 |
| Spaghetti Carbonara | 1000 | 50 |
| Spaghetti Marinara | 680 | 35 |
| Spaghetti Napoletana | 650 | 32 |
| Venetian Chicken | 450 | 18 |

### Desserts per serving

| | | |
|---|---|---|
| Cassata | 150 | 8 |

| | Calories | Fat (g) |
|---|---|---|
| *Figs* | 60 | 1 |
| *Profiteroles* | 500 | 30 |

## KENTUCKY FRIED CHICKEN – All per item

| | | |
|---|---|---|
| *Fillet Burger* | 409 | 17 |
| *Zinger Burger* | 440 | 19 |
| *Fillet Tower* | 575 | 28 |
| *Zinger Tower* | 607 | 31 |
| *Drum* | 186 | 11 |
| *Thigh* | 288 | 20 |
| *Wing* | 200 | 13 |
| *Twister* | 541 | 30 |
| *Crispy Strip* | 113 | 6 |
| *Fries Regular* | 294 | 15 |
| *Fries Large* | 382 | 19 |
| *Corn* | 69 | 2 |

## MCDONALD'S – All per serving

### Breakfast per serving

| | | |
|---|---|---|
| *Bacon & Egg McMuffin* | 346 | 18 |
| *Bacon Roll with Brown Sauce* | 289 | 10 |
| *Big Breakfast* | 591 | 36 |
| *Hash Brown* | 138 | 8 |

| | Calories | Fat (g) |
|---|---|---|
| *Muffin, buttered* | 157 | 4 |
| *Muffin, buttered with preserve* | 234 | 4 |
| *Pancakes & Sausage* | 670 | 27 |
| *Sausage & Egg McMuffin* | 427 | 25 |

## Meals per serving

| | Calories | Fat (g) |
|---|---|---|
| *Big Mac* | 493 | 23 |
| *Cheeseburger* | 299 | 12 |
| *Chicken McNuggets (4)* | 167 | 10 |
| *Chicken McNuggets (6)* | 253 | 15 |
| *Chicken McNuggets (9)* | 379 | 22 |
| *Chicken McNuggets (20)* | 842 | 49 |
| *Double Cheeseburger* | 438 | 22 |
| *Filet-O-Fish* | 389 | 18 |
| *Fish Fingers* | 163 | 7 |
| *Hamburger* | 253 | 8 |
| *McChicken Sandwich* | 375 | 17 |
| *Quarter Pounder* | 423 | 19 |
| *Quarter Pounder with Cheese* | 516 | 27 |
| *French Fries, regular* | 206 | 9 |
| *French Fries, medium* | 293 | 13 |
| *French Fries, large* | 412 | 18 |
| *Vegetable Deluxe* | 423 | 19 |

| | Calories | Fat(g) |
|---|---|---|
| Barbecue Sauce | 55 | 0 |
| Mild Mustard Sauce | 63 | 4 |
| Sweet Curry Sauce | 61 | 1 |
| Sweet & Sour Sauce | 58 | 0 |
| Tomato Ketchup | 26 | 0 |

### Desserts per serving

| | Calories | Fat(g) |
|---|---|---|
| Apple Pie | 230 | 13 |
| Birthday Cake | 250 | 8 |
| Donut, Chocolate | 329 | 19 |
| Donut, Cinnamon | 302 | 18 |
| Donut, Sugared | 303 | 18 |
| Ice Cream Cone | 156 | 5 |
| Ice Cream Cone with Flake | 204 | 8 |
| Sundae, no topping | 219 | 8 |
| Sundae, hot caramel | 358 | 8 |
| Sundae, hot fudge | 351 | 11 |
| Sundae, strawberry | 296 | 8 |

### Drinks per serving

| | Calories | Fat(g) |
|---|---|---|
| Coffee with creamer | 17 | 1 |
| Coca-Cola, regular | 108 | 0 |
| Coca-Cola, medium | 172 | 0 |

| | Calories | Fat (g) |
|---|---|---|
| Coca-Cola, large | 226 | 0 |
| Coca-Cola, extra large | 323 | 0 |
| Diet Coke, regular | 1 | 0 |
| Diet Coke, medium | 2 | 0 |
| Diet Coke, large | 2 | 0 |
| Diet Coke, extra large | 3 | 0 |
| Fanta Orange, regular | 108 | 0 |
| Fanta Orange, medium | 172 | 0 |
| Fanta Orange, large | 226 | 0 |
| Fanta Orange, extra large | 316 | 0 |
| Hot Chocolate Drink | 105 | 3 |
| Milk | 124 | 4 |
| Milkshake, Banana, regular | 396 | 10 |
| Milkshake, Banana, large | 507 | 13 |
| Milkshake, Chocolate, regular | 403 | 10 |
| Milkshake, Chocolate, large | 516 | 13 |
| Milkshake, Strawberry, regular | 403 | 10 |
| Milkshake, Strawberry, large | 512 | 13 |
| Milkshake, Vanilla, regular | 383 | 10 |
| Milkshake, Vanilla, large | 490 | 13 |
| Pure Orange Juice, regular | 94 | 0 |
| Pure Orange Juice, large | 141 | 0 |
| Sprite, regular | 108 | 0 |

| | Calories | Fat (g) |
|---|---|---|
| Sprite, medium | 172 | 0 |
| Sprite, large | 226 | 0 |
| Sprite, extra large | 316 | 0 |
| Tea with skimmed milk | 10 | 1 |

## PIZZA EXPRESS – All per item

### Main Courses per serving

| | Calories | Fat (g) |
|---|---|---|
| Pizza Margherita | 621 | 21 |
| Pizza Napolitana | 650 | 23 |
| Pizza Mushroom | 627 | 21 |
| Pizza Neptune | 604 | 16 |
| Pizza Florentina | 724 | 27 |
| Pizza Veneziana | 613 | 19 |
| Pizza Giardiniera | 711 | 26 |
| Pizza Four Seasons | 720 | 29 |
| Pizza Capricciosa | 755 | 29 |
| Pizza Caprina | 635 | 22 |
| Pizza alle Noci | 766 | 35 |
| Pizza La Reine | 665 | 23 |
| Pizza Siciliana | 723 | 27 |
| Pizza Sloppy Giuseppe | 783 | 33 |
| Pizza American | 753 | 32 |
| Pizza American Hot | 757 | 33 |

| | Calories | Fat (g) |
|---|---|---|
| Pizza Quattro Formaggi | 636 | 22 |
| Pizza Cajun | 822 | 21 |
| Soho Pizza | 690 | 24 |
| King Edward | 670 | 36 |
| Lasagne Pasticciate | 499 | 28 |
| Cannelloni | 630 | 38 |
| Ham & Eggs Pizza Express | 504 | 24 |
| Salade Nicoise | 729 | 37 |
| Mozzarella & Tomato Salad | 623 | 33 |
| Melanzane Parmigiana | 645 | 47 |

### Side Orders per serving

| | Calories | Fat (g) |
|---|---|---|
| Garlic Bread | 227 | 10 |
| Baked Dough Balls | 200 | 2 |
| Mixed Salad | 190 | 18 |
| Mozzarella & Tomato Salad | 281 | 21 |
| Caesar Salad | 426 | 35 |
| Pollo Salad | 557 | 29 |

### Desserts per serving

| | Calories | Fat (g) |
|---|---|---|
| Duomo di Bosco | 155 | 0 |
| Fresh Fruit Salad | 125 | 0 |
| Chocolate Fudge Cake | 395 | 17 |

| | Calories | Fat (g) |
|---|---|---|
| *Pear Tart* | 345 | 18 |
| *Cheesecake* | 346 | 25 |
| *Tiramisu* | 456 | 34 |
| *Cassata* | 192 | 7 |
| *Bombe, Coffee & Hazelnut* | 255 | 14 |
| *Bombe, Chocolate & Pistachio* | 248 | 13 |
| *Bombe, Strawberry & Marsala* | 176 | 6 |
| *Bombe, Chocolate & Vanilla* | 246 | 12 |
| *Tartuffo* | 291 | 16 |
| *Bruschetta* | 387 | 18 |
| *Tonno e Fagioli* | 337 | 17 |

### Dessert accompaniments per serving

| | Calories | Fat (g) |
|---|---|---|
| *Vanilla Ice Cream* | 119 | 7 |
| *Double cream* | 188 | 20 |
| *Mascarpone* | 152 | 15 |

### PIZZA HUT – All per item

| | Calories | Fat (g) |
|---|---|---|
| *Medium Margherita (12") The Italian* | 1746 | 61 |
| *Margherita Medium Pan Pizza* | 1426 | 60 |
| *Ham & Mushroom Medium (12") The Italian* | 1614 | 61 |
| *Hawaiian Medium Pan Pizza* | 1446 | 54 |
| *Meat Feast Medium Pan Pizza* | 1943 | 97 |

| | Calories | Fat (g) |
|---|---|---|
| Meat Feast Medium (12") The Italian | 1944 | 97 |
| Supreme Medium Pan Pizza | 1744 | 87 |
| Supreme Medium (12") The Italian | 1782 | 88 |
| Stuffed Crust Original Margherita | 2626 | 98 |
| The Edge The Veggie | 2176 | 89 |
| The Edge The Works | 2576 | 128 |
| The Edge The Meaty | 3307 | 186 |
| Garlic Bread (4 pieces) | 386 | 20 |
| Chicken Wings (6) | 466 | 33 |
| Chicken Wings with BBQ Dip | 514 | 33 |
| Chicken Wings with Sour Cream & Chive Dip | 678 | 56 |
| Garlic Mushrooms (12) | 215 | 11 |
| Garlic Mushrooms with BBQ Dip | 263 | 11 |
| Garlic Mushrooms with Sour Cream & Chives | 427 | 34 |
| Jacket Skins (4) | 570 | 37 |
| Jacket Skins with BBQ Dip | 618 | 37 |
| Jacket Skins with Sour Cream & Chive Dip | 782 | 60 |

**Dessert per serving**

| | | |
|---|---|---|
| Dairy Ice Cream | 272 | 13 |

# HAVING A DRINK

Beware the demon drink! Alcohol is loaded with calories. If you are drinking soft drinks or mixers and spirits, ask for the low-calorie versions – the regular versions have up to a hundred times as many calories.

www.slimfast.co.uk

| | Calories | Fat (g) |
|---|---|---|

## BEERS

### Draught Beers – per 1/2 pint, 284ml

| | Calories | Fat (g) |
|---|---|---|
| Bass | 128 | 0 |
| Beamish | 90 | 0 |
| Courage | 100 | 0 |
| Double Diamond | 90 | 0 |
| Ind Coope | 80 | 0 |
| John Bull | 85 | 0 |
| John Smith's | 95 | 0 |
| London Pride | 105 | 0 |
| Ruddles | 100 | 0 |
| Stones | 90 | 0 |
| Walkers | 80 | 0 |
| Webster's | 90 | 0 |

### Canned Beers – per 440ml can

| | Calories | Fat (g) |
|---|---|---|
| Beamish | 150 | 0 |
| Burton's | 180 | 0 |
| Double Diamond | 165 | 0 |
| John Smith's | 160 | 0 |
| McEwans Scotch Ale | 365 | 0 |
| Tartan | 138 | 0 |
| Tetley | 140 | 0 |

| | Calories | Fat (g) |
|---|---|---|
| *Worthington's* | *120* | *0* |

## Bottled Beers

| | | |
|---|---|---|
| *Bentley (284ml)* | *80* | *0* |
| *Ind Coope (275ml)* | *75* | *0* |
| *Newcastle Brown (440ml)* | *165* | *0* |

## LAGERS

### Draught Lagers – per 1/2 pint, 284ml

| | | |
|---|---|---|
| *Budweiser* | *110* | *0* |
| *Foster's* | *90* | *0* |
| *Hofmeister* | *85* | *0* |
| *Holsten Export* | *115* | *0* |
| *Kronenbourg* | *120* | *0* |
| *Tennent's* | *95* | *0* |

### Canned Lagers – per 440ml can

| | | |
|---|---|---|
| *Carling Black Label* | *198* | *0* |
| *Castlemaine XXXX* | *165* | *0* |
| *Foster's* | *185* | *0* |
| *Hofmeister* | *130* | *0* |
| *Holsten Pils* | *170* | *0* |
| *Kestrel* | *115* | *0* |

| | Calories | Fat (g) |
|---|---|---|
| *Kestrel Super Strength* | 330 | 0 |
| *Kronenbourg* | 185 | 0 |
| *Lamot Pils* | 165 | 0 |
| *Lowenbrau Special* | 198 | 0 |
| *Skol Extra Strength* | 310 | 0 |
| *Stella Artois* | 185 | 0 |
| *Tennent's* | 140 | 0 |
| *Tennent's Super* | 320 | 0 |

### Bottled Lagers

| | Calories | Fat (g) |
|---|---|---|
| *Carlsberg (275ml)* | 125 | 0 |
| *Carlsberg Special Brew (275ml)* | 205 | 0 |
| *Heineken (275ml)* | 129 | 0 |

### Low & No Alcohol Beers & Lagers

| | Calories | Fat (g) |
|---|---|---|
| *Carlton (1/2 pint 284ml draught)* | 50 | 0 |
| *LA Bitter (275ml bottle)* | 65 | 0 |
| *McEwans LA (440ml can)* | 65 | 0 |
| *Miller Lite (1/2 pint 284ml draught)* | 88 | 0 |
| *Miller Lite (440ml can)* | 136 | 0 |
| *Swan (375ml can)* | 70 | 0 |
| *Swan Light (440ml can)* | 75 | 0 |
| *Tennent's LA (440ml can)* | 80 | 0 |

|  | Calories | Fat(g) |
|---|---|---|
| *White Label (440ml can)* | 135 | 0 |

## CIDERS

### Draught Ciders – per 1/2 pint 284ml

| | Calories | Fat(g) |
|---|---|---|
| *Copperhead* | 85 | 0 |
| *Country Manor, medium dry* | 155 | 0 |
| *Country Manor, medium sweet* | 180 | 0 |
| *Country Manor, sparkling* | 170 | 0 |
| *Merrydown Country* | 140 | 0 |
| *Merrydown Traditional* | 130 | 0 |
| *Merrydown Vintage* | 170 | 0 |
| *Merrydown Vintage Dry* | 150 | 0 |
| *Strongbow* | 101 | 0 |
| *Woodpecker* | 100 | 0 |

### Bottled Ciders – per 275ml bottle

| | Calories | Fat(g) |
|---|---|---|
| *Blackthorn* | 95 | 0 |
| *Diamond White* | 145 | 0 |
| *Red Rock* | 135 | 0 |
| *Taunton Cool* | 95 | 0 |

| | Calories | Fat (g) |
|---|---|---|
| **WINES** – per 115ml glass | | |
| White, dry | 75 | 0 |
| White, sweet | 105 | 0 |
| Red, dry | 80 | 0 |
| Red, sweet | 100 | 0 |
| Rosé | 85 | 0 |
| Sparkling | 90 | 0 |
| Champagne | 80 | 0 |
| | | |
| **Fortified Wines** – per 50ml glass | | |
| Port, red | 70 | 0 |
| Port, vintage | 80 | 0 |
| Sherry, cream | 63 | 0 |
| Sherry, medium | 59 | 0 |
| Sherry, dry | 58 | 0 |
| Sherry, sweet | 68 | 0 |
| | | |
| **SPIRITS & VERMOUTHS** – per 25ml | | |
| Armagnac | 55 | 0 |
| Calvados | 55 | 0 |
| Cognac | 55 | 0 |
| Dark Rum | 55 | 0 |
| Gin | 50 | 0 |

| | Calories | Fat (g) |
|---|---|---|
| *Kentucky Bourbon* | 70 | 0 |
| *Jack Daniels* | 60 | 0 |
| *Martini Bianco* | 34 | 0 |
| *Martini Extra Dry* | 34 | 0 |
| *Martini Rosso* | 47 | 0 |
| *Martini Sweet* | 38 | 0 |
| *Napoleon Brandy* | 56 | 0 |
| *Pernod* | 61 | 0 |
| *Pimms* | 49 | 0 |
| *Spanish Brandy* | 65 | 0 |
| *Southern Comfort* | 70 | 0 |
| *Vodka* | 50 | 0 |
| *Whisky* | 50 | 0 |
| *White Rum* | 52 | 0 |

## LIQUEURS – per 25ml

| | Calories | Fat (g) |
|---|---|---|
| *Advocaat* | 68 | 2 |
| *Amaretto* | 80 | 0 |
| *Benedictine* | 90 | 0 |
| *Cassis* | 65 | 0 |
| *Cointreau* | 78 | 0 |
| *Drambuie* | 85 | 0 |
| *Grand Marnier* | 78 | 0 |

| | Calories | Fat (g) |
|---|---|---|
| *Kirsch* | 50 | 0 |
| *Tia Maria* | 79 | 0 |

## SOFT DRINKS & MIXERS – per 330ml

| | Calories | Fat (g) |
|---|---|---|
| *Bitter Lemon (Schweppes)* | 109 | 0 |
| *Caffeine Free Diet Coke (Coca-Cola)* | 0 | 0 |
| *Cherry Coke (Coca-Cola)* | 140 | 0 |
| *Coca Cola* | 135 | 0 |
| *Diet Coke (Coca-Cola)* | 0 | 0 |
| *Diet Fanta* | 10 | 0 |
| *Diet Lemonade* | 6 | 0 |
| *Lemonade (Tesco)* | 45 | 0 |
| *Orange Juice* | 119 | 0 |
| *Pineapple Juice* | 135 | 0 |
| *Grapefruit Juice* | 109 | 0 |
| *Russchian (Schweppes)* | 73 | 0 |
| *Tonic Water* | 109 | 0 |
| *Soda Water (Schweppes)* | 0 | 0 |
| *Sweetened Grapefruit Juice (Schweppes)* | 120 | 0 |
| *Tomato Juice* | 46 | 0 |